A GUIDE TO EVERYDAY ECONOMIC THINKING

Dedication

For tolerating our spending
    precious vacation days at the writing desk of a summer cabin,
    and untold family hours in front of the computer screen, and
for Kimberly Clayton's conscientious proofreading of the umpteenth
    manuscript,
we dedicate this book to our generous families.

M. G. G.

G. E. C.

A GUIDE TO EVERYDAY ECONOMIC THINKING

Martin Gerhard Giesbrecht
Northern Kentucky University

Gary E. Clayton
Northern Kentucky University

Irwin
McGraw-Hill

Boston, Massachusetts   Burr Ridge, Illinois   Dubuque, Iowa
Madison, Wisconsin   New York, New York
San Francisco, California   St. Louis, Missouri

Irwin/McGraw-Hill
  A Division of The McGraw-Hill Companies

A GUIDE TO EVERYDAY ECONOMIC THINKING

Copyright © 1997 by The McGraw-Hill Companies, Inc. All rights reserved. Printed in the United States of America. Except as permitted under the United States Copyright Act of 1976, no part of this publication may be reproduced or distributed in any form or by any means, or stored in a data base or retrieval system, without the prior written permission of the publisher.

This book is printed on acid-free paper.

1 2 3 4 5 6 7 8 9 0 DOC DOC 9 0 0 9 8 7

ISBN 0-07-011990-2

Publisher: Gary Burke
Sponsoring editor: Lucille Sutton
Productions supervisor: Louis Swaim
Printer: R. R. Donnelley & Sons, Crawfordsville

http://www.mhhe.com

About the Authors

Martin Gerhard Giesbrecht teaches economics at Northern Kentucky University. He has taught and/or conducted research at Stanford University, the University of Chicago, Harvard University, Indiana University, National Chengchi University (Taiwan), Rutgers University, and Wilmington College. His doctoral degree (cum laude) was earned at the University of Munich, Germany, which he attended on a Fulbright Grant. Making economics accessible, intellectually enlightening, and even entertaining is the mission of Martin Giesbrecht's professional life. All of his ten books, including this one, and his many shorter articles, some of which have also appeared in German and Chinese, are dedicated to that end, as is his weekly commentary on WNKU.

Because he writes and speaks in a way that people can understand, the Society of Professional Journalism bestowed its Award for Excellence on him in 1993. He has also won awards from the German-American Chamber of Commerce, the National Aeronautics and Space Administration (NASA), the American Society for Engineering Education, the National Science Foundation, The General Electric Foundation, the Ford Foundation, the U.S. Small Business Administration, and the National Endowment for the Humanities, among others.

Gary E. Clayton teaches economics and finance at Northern Kentucky University. He received his Ph.D. in Economics from the University of Utah, has taught economics and finance at several universities, and has authored and edited a number of books and articles in educational, professional, and technical journals. Dr. Clayton has appeared on a number of radio and television programs and, along with his colleague, Dr. Martin Giesbrecht, has appeared as a guest commentator for "Marketplace," which is broadcast on American Public Radio and originates at the University of Southern California.

Dr. Clayton has a long-standing interest in economic education. He has participated in and directed numerous economic education workshops, received an Outstanding Citizen Certificate of Recognition from the state of Arkansas for his work in economic education, and was a national award winner in the college division of the International Paper Company competition which is sponsored by EconomicsAmerica, the National Council on Economic Education. He also writes for the high school market and currently authors the best-selling principles of economics textbook in the country.

Table of Contents

CHAPTER 1: DECISIONS, DECISIONS
Heroic Decisions	1
Threshold Decisions	2
Incremental Decisions	3
Strategies	4
Thinking Like an Economist	6

CHAPTER 2: BENEFITS AND COSTS
The Price of Everything	7
Utilities	8
The Law of Diminishing Marginal Returns	9
Opportunity Costs	10
Thinking Like an Economist	12

CHAPTER 3: THE MOST BANG FOR THE BUCK
Making Every Hour Count	13
Optimizing Our Resource "Budget"	16
The Elusive Equilibrium	17
Thinking Like an Economist	19

CHAPTER 4: BUSINESS SUCCESS
The Bottom Line	21
Optimizing with Marginal Analysis	22
The "Golden Rule"	24
Thinking Like an Economist	27

CHAPTER 5: PRICES AND MARKETS
A Win-Win Situation	29
Prices as Signals	30
Supply and Demand	31
Market Dynamics	34
Imperfect Markets	35
Thinking Like an Economist	37

CHAPTER 6: THE GAINS FROM TRADE

The Grand Panacea	39
The Law of Comparative Advantage	40
The Welfare Effects of Trade	41
Opposition to Trade	43
Foreign Currency Exchange Rates	44
Thinking Like an Economist	47

CHAPTER 7: GOVERNMENT AND ECONOMICS

Private vs. Public Goods	49
Individual vs. Public Decisions	50
Externalities	52
The Federal Budget	53
Discretionary Fiscal Policy	55
Mandatory Spending?	57
Thinking Like an Economist	59

CHAPTER 8: MONEY AND MONETARY POLICY

Dollars and Cents	61
The Federal Reserve System	62
Monetary Policy	65
Thinking Like an Economist	68

CHAPTER 9: MEASURING ECONOMIC PERFORMANCE

How We Got Here From There	70
The Search for Leading Indicators	70
Finding Safety in Numbers	72
What About the Level of Economic Activity?	74
GDP And All That	75
Thinking Like an Economist	76

CHAPTER 10: WORKING FOR A LIVING

Wealth vs. Work	77
Our Pay Scale	78
Labor Unions	80
Thinking Like an Economist	81

CHAPTER 11: THE ENVIRONMENT

Time Out For A Brief Physics Lesson	83
Pollution and Resource Exhaustion	84
The Incentive to Pollute	86
Internalizing the External Costs	86
If Only Everything Were That Easy!	89
Thinking Like a (Modern) Economist	90

CHAPTER 12: POVERTY

The Mainstream	93
The Emerging Middle Class	94
Defining Poverty	95
A Recipe For Poverty	96
Can Poverty Be Prevented?	97
Thinking Like an Economist	99

CHAPTER 13: THE ECONOMICS OF CRIME

The Nature of Crime	101
When Crime Pays	102
A Bad Situation Can Get Worse	103
Victimless Crimes	104
Thinking Like an Economist	105

CHAPTER 14: ECONOMIC SYSTEMS AND INSTITUTIONS

Families	107
Proprietorships and Partnerships	109
Corporations	110
Governments Again	112
Central Planning	113
Thinking Like an Economist	116

INDEX   119

Preface

Of all the interests, enthusiasms, arts, sciences, professions, and vocations that humans pursue on this planet, only some focus directly on ourselves, as the primary subject. Among those that do–and the list includes such diversities as medicine and sports–one of the most important is economics.

The focus of economics is concentrated on us, because every one of us is touched by economic considerations every day of our lives. Especially when we are making the many large and small decisions required of us as consumers, producers, business managers, employees, family members, parents, friends, members of groups and communities, political leaders, and citizens, our behavior is powerfully influenced by economic considerations; considerations derived from the economic way of thinking.

But, what constitutes "the economic way of thinking?" From all of the thousands of things that economists say and do, what are the common threads that tie the majority of their efforts together? And, perhaps most important of all, why is the perspective of the economist even important? If we can provide satisfactory answers to these questions, then we will have accomplished our mission. This is what our little book sets out to do.

The key phenomena of economic thinking is making a choice, and rational choices are not made in a vacuum. Accurate and sufficient information is needed, the relevant costs and benefits of the various alternatives must be compared, and previous experience has to be taken into account, as do our aspirations for the future. Description, analysis, explanation, calculation, and–riskiest of all–prediction are among the tactics employed. Throughout all, both the process and the product must be humane; anything less would hardly be economic thinking.

Despite the broad outlines presented above, this is not a textbook on or a survey of economics. It is much too short for that. Economic science has grown vast in the past century, and some branches have become quite abstruse and mathematical. Economic institutions and economic practices, especially in the realms of management, commerce, finance, and public policy, have also become complex and sophisticated. The result is literally thousands of books and journals that collectively encompass the subject today.

But running through all of it, as a unifying theme, is our economic way of thinking. This is, after all, the primary focus of all of economics; this is what all the rest of economics endeavors to support. And this is also what is most useful about economics, because every one of us, every day of our lives, can benefit from the economic way of thinking.

Martin Gerhard Giesbrecht
Gary E. Clayton
1997

Chapter 1

DECISIONS, DECISIONS

> *The trouble with economics is that it will not stand still. Issues change, ideas change, understanding changes. Even the past does not look exactly the same from one year to the next and the present is apt to alter almost out of all recognition... Economics is a large subject, and the first problem that confronts us is how to approach it, how to get hold of the thing.*
>
> – Robert L. Heilbroner (1919–), American economist and educator

When the happy day finally arrives, and the church organist is laying down the first few sonorous chords of the wedding march, we may wonder when or how it was that we actually decided to get married. And whenever or however it was, it was a heroic decision, so called not because only heroes and heroines get married, but because the decision requires heroic behavior.

Heroic Decisions

A heroic decision, in this context, is essentially a giant leap in the dark: requiring one to make a bold, daring, and largely irreversible choice, often on the basis of very little information. Decisions to pull a child from the path of an oncoming car, to storm the enemy on the battlefield, to get a tattoo, and to become pregnant are, therefore, in the same category. Heroic decisions are in many ways unique decisions, with profound and long-lasting outcomes. And, once we've acted, it is extremely difficult to go back on the decision.

In spite of this, heroic decisions are often attractive. They are the stuff of excitement and romance. Fiction writers construct their novels of such decision situations, and our society tends to support and celebrate them. Heroes are honored for their courage. Newlyweds are cheered and bestowed with wedding presents. Family and friends show love and concern for newly pregnant mothers-to-be.

But heroic decisions are mostly outside the scope of economic thinking. They are taken on the basis of relatively little useful information about all the pros and cons involved, they go forth with very little rational analysis of this information, and no opportunity for trial and error exists. The risks are usually either unknown or very high. Heroic decisions make life interesting, but they are not the best way to make everyday decisions.

Threshold Decisions

Perhaps a more rational type of decision is what can be called a threshold decision. We take a tiny sip of our beverage, to see if it isn't too hot to drink; we taste a new food, to see if it agrees with our palate; we accept a trial subscription to a magazine, before we order it for a whole year; and so on. If the outcome is satisfactory, if it has satisfied some minimum threshold of comfort, taste or convenience– we gulp the beverage, we purchase a quantity of the food, and we order the magazine subscription for a whole year.

Many business decisions are made this way. In particular, businesses often employ capital budgeting techniques to evaluate the profitability of an expansion or a change in the way the firm produces its product or conducts its affairs. To do so, the firm gathers all useful and relevant information to the situation–including the impact of the decision on the future costs and revenues of the firm. Next, the profitability of the proposal is estimated and then compared with some threshold requirement. The firm may, for example, set a threshold or hurdle requirement of a (say) 20 percent annual return for new investments. All proposals that that fall below the threshold return are rejected; all proposals that meet or exceed the threshold are accepted.

Despite the popularity of threshold decisions, they have significant drawbacks. One is that they tend to group alternatives in broad categories when in fact the differences between some choices may not be all that significant. For example, the firm with the 20 percent return threshold would reject an investment with an anticipated return of 19.99 percent, whereas it would accept a project with a 20.01 percent return, even though there is little difference between the two alternatives. (Students are familiar with this type of distinction when it comes to receiving end-of-semester grades. While there may be little numerical difference between a C- and a D+, the former is a passing grade whereas the latter may mean that the course must be repeated.)

Another difficulty with threshold decisions is that they may not always be flexible enough to take into account the ever-changing environment in the real world. A threshold might be relevant today, but will it be appropriate tomorrow? The threshold can always be changed, of course, but the nature of the threshold decision is that a lot of future action (or inaction) takes place on the basis of a single decision made today.

Incremental Decisions

An even more useful type of decision is called an *incremental*, or *marginal* decision. Like the case of the threshold decision, as much useful information as practicable should gathered so that it can be thoroughly and accurately analyzed. Then, the resulting decision should be as incrementally small as possible, so that, if it turns out to be bad, it can be reversed, and not too much will be lost. If it turns out to be a good decision, it can be repeated. But again only a small, incremental step should be taken, so that as many options as possible for alternative decisions remain available.

A cook, for example, might experiment with a recipe by adding a little more of a single ingredient to see how it affects the texture and flavor of a meal. If the experiment is successful, even more of the ingredient could be added in stages until the outcome was determined to be detrimental rather than beneficial. The rational business firm behaves much in the same manner. One ingredient of the production process, labor (perhaps in the form of a single worker), could be added to see if total output, and hence total revenue, increases enough to warrant the extra cost. If the experiment is successful, the firm would add another worker, and then even another, until such time as the benefits gained were not worth the cost.

Economists call such decisions marginal decisions, because they deal with each salami slice of behavior separately, on the thin margin between past and future. By using this word, they definitely do not imply that marginal decisions are somehow unimportant or trivial. In fact, economists argue that marginal decisions are the best kind because they emphasize useful information and, by not taking a larger leap into the future than necessary, the direction of the decisions can be changed.

All of us make good use of marginal decisions every day. Even some of the traditionally heroic decisions, such as getting married or getting a tattoo, may be gradually becoming more marginal these days. In regard to marriage, long engagements and premarital cohabitation enable couples to gather lots of information about themselves. Reworded marriage vows and prenuptial agreements analyze and encode this information rationally. And easy divorces make the vows reversible. (Conservatives and romantics are appalled!) In regard to tattoos, cheap temporary stick-ons are now on the market. They wash off in a few days.

Strategies

Few decisions are one-shot affairs. Frequently, we encounter situations that develop over a period of time, that produce a flow of new information during that time, and that, therefore, require a series of sequential decisions, each based on the outcomes of the preceding decisions and on the new information available. Such situations call for strategies.

Strategies or decision rules, as they are sometimes called, specify in advance how decisions are to be made for all successive stages of a developing situation, given what has gone before and what is known at the moment. Uncertainty about these developments is why strategies are required. If we knew for sure how all eventualities will fall into place, we could simply make complete decisions covering everything ahead of time. But we don't, so we need strategies.

The specificity of strategies can vary. At one extreme, a strategy can presume to have accounted for all contingencies and have established a best choice decision for each. Some chess playing computer programs presume this precision. At the other extreme is the "let's cross this bridge when we come to it" mentality. It, too, is a strategy, but an often oversimplified one. Good functional strategies for real-life applications lie somewhere between these extremes.

As difficult as it may seem to make decision rules about situations that develop in, as yet, unknown ways in an uncertain future, there are ways to make such strategies practical and useful. First of all, many eventualities in dynamic situations are sufficiently similar to enable the decision maker to choose the same decision each time with some confidence. Those maddening tic-tac-toe players, who can almost never be made to lose a game, have mastered such a set of decision rules. Good sales persons, winning politicians, and champion fly casting anglers almost certainly also base their successes on such repertoires of tried and true decision rules. Actually, we all have such repertoires. And, like everybody, we have to be careful not to let these handy decision rules become mindless habits or stupid prejudices.

Secondly, as the information continues to accumulate in dynamic situations, some uncertainties disappear and others begin to diminish. Taking advantage of these developments is, in fact, the main justification for using strategies, instead of once-and-for-all decisions. As the decision situation for which a strategy has been created nears its conclusion, less and less of it remains in the uncertain future. This means that, in its last stages, a strategy can focus more and more accurately on its target. Similarly, the accumulating experience acquired by running the strategy enables the decision maker to attach actual probabilities to future events that were only vague possibilities before. A little caution about presumed precision is well advised here, however. We all know how unreliable the TV weather forecaster's "eighty percent chance of rain" often is.

Thinking Like an Economist

Everyday economic thinking, as you may have gathered, is based on rational decision making that is implemented in small, incremental steps. Of course, there are other elements to consider, but these will be introduced as we go along. For now, we start with the nature of decisions and the way they fit into our overall decision making framework.

From the many types of decisions available, economists are prone to reject the romantically attractive heroic decisions because they deny us the freedom to experiment with a sufficient number of alternatives. Threshold decisions are an improvement, but they encourage us to go a long way without providing for a check on our progress. Instead, economists prefer the incremental, or marginal, decisions which allow us to test and then evaluate decisions in very small steps.

The trouble with economics, as Heilbroner correctly observed, "is that it (economics) will not stand still." However, we need to recognize that a changing world makes the economic way of thinking even more useful because it becomes the one constant that helps us interpret, understand, and navigate our changing environment. Change is a fact of life, and the future stands in front of us like some vast uncharted sea. Successful navigation requires a strategy–*an economic way of thinking*–to help us get from here to there.

Chapter 2

BENEFITS AND COSTS

> *I conceive that the great part of the miseries of mankind are brought upon them by false estimates they have made of the value of things.*
> –Benjamin Franklin (1706-1790), American statesman and author

Wouldn't it be convenient if all things in this world had a clearly marked price sticker, something that would show benefits as well as costs? Then we could compare the values of them all, not just the usually priced things, such as clothes, groceries, the telephone bill, rent, taxes, and our own wage rate. We could also compare those currently unpriced things, both positive–such as the moonlight on a summer evening, the breeze on a nearby beach–or negative, such as mowing the yard or filling out our annual income tax forms.

The Price of Everything

As ubiquitous as money prices are, in our commercialized and industrialized economies, probably well over half of all the values in our lives have no obvious dollars-and-cents value. That doesn't mean that these values aren't important. Some of the positive ones, such as freedom, love, and beauty, are, perhaps, the most enriching things in our lives; and some of the negative ones, such as sickness, hatred, and jealousy, can diminish our welfare more than almost anything else.

So, if we are going to make decisions involving nonpriced values–and all of us do–then we have to guess at their values somehow. In fact, we have to guess at the values of the priced goods too, because their prices only reflect market values, not the use values of the goods to ourselves. Indeed, if we didn't estimate the use value to ourselves of an item to be larger than its price, we wouldn't buy it. (After all, why bother to buy an item if we place a higher value on the money that we would have to give up, than on the item to be received?)

Utilities

Lacking a better term, economists call this estimated use value of an item its *utility* (and the estimated negative value its *disutility*), although satisfaction or benefit may be better terms in some situations. Returns, meaning anything the item does for us, has a nice neutral ring to it, but utility is the term of choice among economists. In fact, in the early 1900s, economists often ascribed numerical values to utility, as if it were a countable quantity. While this might seem odd, people sometimes do the same thing when they rate otherwise immeasurable quantities numerically. For example, someone might use a rating scale of one to ten to define how good something tastes, how much they enjoyed a particular movie, or even to describe the attractiveness of another person.

All of these are attempts to enumerate quantities that don't readily lend themselves to precise measurement. In fact, modern economists think of utility in terms of being an ordinal (rank order), rather than a cardinal (measurable), form of ranking. That is, we would *not* say that we received two units of utility (or "utils") from one experience and a value of three from another. Instead, and in terms of ordinal measurement (the way we measure utility), we would regard a value of three as simply bigger or better than two, but not quite as good as a value of four. This may seem a bit mushy and imprecise to the non-economist, but it turns out that an extraordinary body of pure economic theory is built entirely on ordinal measures.

Here's a little illustration that shows the usefulness of ordinal comparisons. Suppose that, as part of a lottery prize, you are allowed to choose one of three boxes that are stuffed with one hundred dollar bills. One box is large, one is medium, and one is small. You probably wouldn't have to think twice (nor would you have to know exactly how much bigger the large box was than the small box) in order for you to make your choice–even though the terms "large," "medium," and "small" are all ordinal measures.

For our purposes here, the fact that utility is subjective and therefore cannot be measured is not really a problem. Most of the time we just feel these utilities in our bones.

The Law of Diminishing Marginal Returns

In all of this estimation of use values, one thing is certain: as more and more of one kind of item is encountered, a point is always reached when each additional unit of that item gives us less positive utility (i.e. satisfaction) than the preceding item. That is, a satiation effect begins to set in. Sooner or later we are tempted to declare, "Enough, already!" This is called the "Law of Eventually Diminishing Marginal Returns," or the "Law of Diminishing Returns" for short.

The two diagrams below illustrate this situation. The figure on the left shows how marginal returns might decline for an individual as more and more of an activity is pursued (a service utilized or a product consumed). The diagram on the right shows how the total returns for the individual are cumulative in the sense that total returns are the sum of the marginal returns:

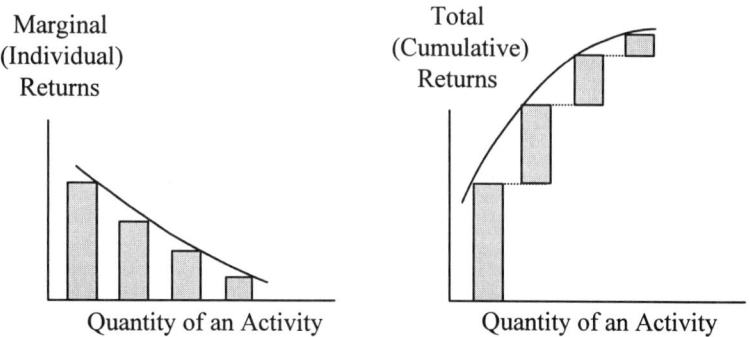

So, whether we view the activity from the perspective of the returns from each individual incremental unit of behavior, or from the perspective of the accruing cumulative returns from the incremental units of behavior, the story is always the same: the incremental returns diminish.

The law of eventually diminishing marginal returns seems to be one of our universe's basic truths, like the Law of Gravity, the Law of Conservation of Matter and Energy, and the Law of Entropy. We encounter it hundreds of times a day–when we have had enough sleep, enough of each kind of food we are eating that day, enough time spent working, enough time spent in front of the TV, and so on and on–but the law is far from trivial. By making it impossible to accomplish all things with just one ingredient or just one activity, the law of eventually diminishing marginal returns explains the complexity of many processes.

Furthermore, life's activities and experiences can yield negative returns, as well as positive ones. A hike in the mountains on a beautiful day may seem to yield overwhelmingly positive pleasure for the first hour or two, and so we hardly notice our backpacks or our heavy boots. But, with passing time, the backpack grows heavier, the body begins to tire, and the positive marginal returns become smaller and smaller. Eventually, the boots begin to ache our feet, and the last mile becomes a grueling pain. Once we've reached the point where we decide we've had enough, that the trip from this point on is simply too long, the marginal returns become negative and the total returns from the activity begin to decrease. The secret to maximizing our total returns, then, is to enjoy all of the marginal returns we can, without actually reaching the point where they become negative.

Opportunity Costs

In the many large and small decisions we have to make in everyday life, every action has its own unique cost or consequence. And, because these costs or consequences must be considered before the decision is made, it helps to simplify their estimation as much as possible. So instead of trying to generate monetary equivalents for all the nonmonetary costs, we can simply ask ourselves, "What is the best alternative use of the money, time, and effort we are proposing to spend?" Or, to put it another way, "What are we forfeiting by doing what we propose to do?" Whatever this alternative is, whatever it is that we have to forfeit, that is the real total cost–the *opportunity cost*, as economists like to call it–of our proposed activity.

We approach the problem in this manner because costs go far beyond dollars and cents outlays. For example, the costs of going to college include more than the tuition fee and all attendant monetary expenses, such as books, laboratory fees, transportation and parking, and room and board. They also include the time and effort it takes to be a student. And they include the costs of not being able to work at a full time job, not being able to relax with old, pre-college friends, and not being able to afford some of the amenities–a nicer car, some newer clothes, a trip with the family–because so much money, time, and effort is going for college.

If accurate money equivalents could be estimated for all the nonmonetary costs involved, careful accounting could come up with a numerical total for the real cost of a college education. This sum could then be set against a similarly estimated numerical total real benefit of a college education, and the difference between the two totals will show whether or not college is worthwhile. Such processes, dignified by the name cost-benefit analyses, are widely used to evaluate all kinds of projects and endeavors, including new construction projects, research proposals, and government programs. Whole new professions have grown up specializing in dealing with the often nonmonetary environmental impacts and social consequences that are factored into such thorough cost-benefit analyses.

Of course, anyone with an imagination can probably think of dozens of alternatives to every proposed activity. But we can't do all of them at once, so only the most valuable alternative–the one that is most costly *not* to do–is the one that establishes true opportunity cost. And, as always, we have to be honest with ourselves. We wouldn't want to use an opportunity cost that is unrealistic. For example, the opportunity cost of going to college is unlikely to be having to forego being elected President of the United States. But if we are honest, realistic, and thoughtful, and if we remember the immutable law of eventually diminishing marginal returns, we will be able to weigh utilities against opportunity costs and come up with good, rational, economically sound decisions.

Thinking Like an Economist

The message intended in all this, then, is that accurate, clear-headed, and well-informed economic calculation goes far beyond a mere accounting of dollars and cents. The old saying, that "an economist is a person who knows the price of everything and the value of nothing," is not only a bum rap, but it is 180 degrees off the mark. Prices and costs–moneys, in general–are important, of course, but only because of the various things they represent.

So, to be economically realistic, the true value of anything is what it is worth to us when compared to the nearest available alternative. This "opportunity cost" way of thinking applies universally both to incomes and to expenditures, to benefits and costs, and to all of life's pleasures and life's pains. And, while it seems to simplify our calculus of value determination, it actually makes it much more profound and much more personal and realistic. That is, the nearest available alternatives that serve as the bases for comparisons are necessarily our own available alternatives, not somebody else's. And they have to be realistic alternatives, not some theoretical or philosophical ideal.

Finally, all this economic calculation takes place in a dynamic and changing environment, and it is largely our own behavior that drives the dynamic and causes the changes. Our ongoing activity, after all, is what causes the marginal returns from this activity eventually to diminish and the marginal costs of this activity eventually to increase. So nothing is finally settled, at least, not for long. The requirement that we continue to think like an economist continues, on and on.

Chapter 3

THE MOST BANG FOR THE BUCK

> *Economics is significant, then, not merely because it investigates an important slice of life in the market place, but because the phenomena which emerge in a relatively clear and quantitative form in the market place are also found in virtually all other human activities.*
>
> Kenneth Boulding (1910-1993), American economist

The problem is the long reach of the law of eventually diminishing marginal returns. It makes life complicated. If it weren't for that law, we could find the one thing that we like to do best and just keep doing it over and over, more and more. Our happiness would increase continually, surpassing contentment, surpassing the state of glee, and ultimately even surpassing ecstasy.

Making Every Hour Count

The cold truth is that no such endlessly wonderful activity exists. In our real world, all positive returns eventually diminish on the margin, as we do anything over and over, more and more. And long before the marginal returns from any one activity diminish very much, the opportunity cost–the value of another activity foregone, because we are doing the one activity–begins to loom larger in our awareness. We begin to ask ourselves, "Are we doing too much of one thing and not enough of the other?" In other words, the problem is to get the most bang for the buck.

A brief numerical example may clarify this situation. (And we apologize for the numbers, but they are easier to read than a graph.) Suppose, for the sake of simplicity, we are considering only two activities: sleeping and being awake. We enjoy both of them. Here is a hypothetical person's estimated hour-by-hour marginal utility of sleeping, on a scale of one to ten.

Hour: 1 2 3 4 5 6 7 8 9 10 11 12 13 14 15 16 17 18 19 20 21 22 23 24 25 26
Utility: 10 10 9 9 8 8 7 7 6 6 5 5 5 4 4 4 3 3 3 2 2 2 1 1 1 1

The estimated per-hour marginal utilities of sleeping diminish, from ten down to one, as the day goes on, but sleeping still generates some utility, even in hours 25 and 26. However, since a day on this planet only has 24 hours, we have to stop our utility accounting at hour number 24. The total possible utilities per 24-hour day from sleeping, then, is 124, the sum of all the above marginal utilities.

As satisfying as a 124 total utilities count may be, we may suspect that sleeping all day is not the key to maximum happiness. So let's try being awake. Here is a similar marginal utility table for being awake.

Hour: 1 2 3 4 5 6 7 8 9 10 11 12 13 14 15 16 17 18 19 20 21 22 23 24 25 26
Utility: 10 10 10 10 10 9 9 9 9 9 8 8 8 8 7 7 7 6 6 6 5 5 5 4 4 3

Again the estimated per-hour (marginal) utilities diminish as the day goes on. Yet, they don't diminish very fast, and, if the day had more than 24 hours, the total of these utilities would easily exceed 185 (the total for the first 24 hours), so being awake seems to give us better returns than being asleep.

Does that mean we should choose to stay awake all day, every day, rather than to sleep? (Stupid question!) Obviously not. All human beings on this Earth opt for mixing sleep and being awake in some proportion. And what would be the best proportion for our hypothetical human being whose marginal utilities tables are given above? He or she can find that easily, pretty much the way we do it in real life, by progressing sequentially through the 24 hours, and choosing whatever activity generates the most utilities for each hour.

Here is one of several possible results. It begins with being awake. (If we begin with being asleep, the day's pattern of sleep and being awake would be different, but the proportions of both would be the same.) Both of our utility tables are reproduced below for convenience, with the addition of a combined sleeping/awake schedule in the center of the illustration where "A" stands for being awake and "S" stands for sleeping.

We start by observing that a person would prefer to spend the first five hours awake, where each hour generates 10 units of utility. When the sixth hour arrives, the individual has a choice–to continue to stay awake for the sixth hour (and enjoy 9 units of utility), or to enjoy the first hour of sleep (which generates 10 units of utility). If the individual chooses to sleep, the logical choice would be to sleep for a total of four hours and accumulate utilities 10, 10, 9, and 9 respectively. A fifth hour of sleep (the 10th hour of the day) would generate only 8 units of utility, which is less than could be obtained by awakening and enjoying 9 units of utility.

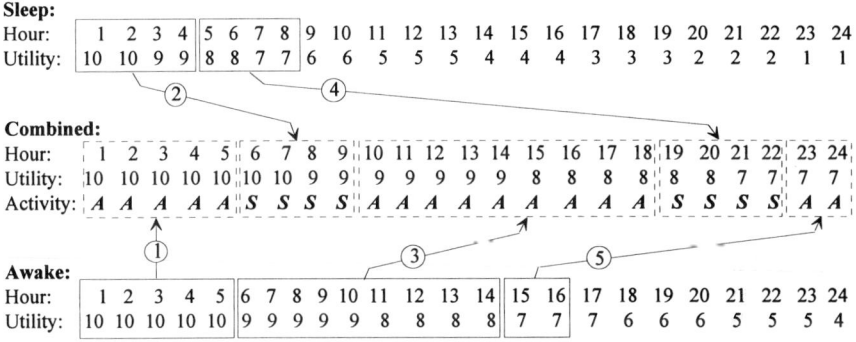

This pattern would continue until the 24-hour day was complete. Given the respective utilities for being awake and sleeping our person chooses to sleep eight hours out of every 24, in two four-hour stints. Newborn children and astronauts tend to mix sleep with being awake a little like this, but most of us would opt for eight hours of sleep in one stint, in order to accommodate ourselves more closely to our planet's day and night cycle, accommodations that would be reflected in the magnitude of the utilities in the tables.

Notice also that the marginal utility of the last hour of being awake in 24 hours, the sixteenth awake hour, which occurs in hour 24, is seven, which is equal to the marginal utility of the last hour of sleep in 24 hours, the eighth sleep hour, occurring in hour 22. This is proof that there is nothing to be gained by switching a little awake time for a little sleep time. In other words, an optimum combination of sleeping and being awake is achieved. Notice also that the total utility from this 24-hour day of mixed sleeping and being awake is now 209, substantially higher than the 124 from just sleeping or the 185 from just being awake.

Finally, notice that the decision to establish an alternating awake/sleep pattern is a result of the economic way of thinking which makes use of incremental decision making. For every hour of the day in the table, the question was, "Which activity, sleeping or staying awake, generates the highest marginal utility?" Every choice that was made was made at the margin, with an eye to amassing the most total utility. Our marginal analysis which is based on subjective measurements helped us discover one of several possible solutions to the awake/sleep pattern. Other patterns are certainly possible–*but no other solution will generate more overall utility.*

Of course, real people don't enumerate estimated utilities for each hour of activity and read the results off tables. We estimate vague, nonnumerical values for the benefits to be derived from alternative activities in the moments, hours, days, and even years to come, and make our choices accordingly. Furthermore, there are many more things to do than merely to sleep or be awake. Budgeting our time, to get the maximum value from it, becomes a major juggling act. What's worse, the more experienced and sophisticated we become, the more alternatives we tend to have, meaning that we have to juggle even more skillfully. Maybe this is what is meant by the saying, "ignorance is bliss."

Finally, if we have a great many alternatives, it may be in our best interests to move from one to another fairly often–or to never do any one of them for very long–so that we never have to settle for significantly diminished marginal returns in any one activity. As a result, our total benefits–profits, returns, utilities, satisfactions–from all activities will be especially high, thus giving us "the most bang for our buck." This is the real payoff for being smart.

Optimizing Our Resource "Budget"

Time is not our only resource. We also have energy; various material assets, such as land, buildings, vehicles, tools, appliances, and so on; various intangible assets, such as skills, experiences, networks of colleagues and friends, and so on. And, of course, we have some large or small quantities of money.

Like time, all of these have value for us only to the degree that we put them to use. Even things we don't use immediately have value for us, through our anticipation of being able to use them later. That's the whole logic behind saving. Furthermore, as stamp collectors and baseball card collectors can tell us, there is a certain joy in simple ownership. In any case, be we rich or poor, the number and variety of things we have to put to use ends up being quite substantial.

And the uses to which these assets can be put are also very numerous. A separate marginal returns table, like either the one for sleeping or the one for being awake shown above, could be generated for each one of our assets being put to each of its varied uses. Even for people of modest enterprise, this could easily come to several hundred such tables. Furthermore, these tables have to be compared simultaneously with one another, as we did with the sleeping and being awake tables, in order to find the best combination of uses that will produce the highest total benefits. All the while, we have to remember that these decisions, like all decisions, are based on estimated returns. Bad estimates usually lead to bad decisions.

Incredible as it may seem, this is what we actually do when we are behaving logically and rationally . . . not with tables of numbers, of course, but with estimates of vague, nonnumerical values for all of these alternatives. Naturally, it behooves us to make these estimates and comparisons as thoroughly and as accurately as possible. All of this is an enormous undertaking and responsibility. At times, it may seem a tedious chore. But it contains the secret of good economic thinking, and it separates the winners from the losers.

The Elusive Equilibrium

We might hope that, after making all these estimates and comparisons thoroughly and accurately, after facing our responsibilities faithfully and completing this giant juggling act of marginal values, we will finally reach an optimum combination of all alternatives that we can enjoy and live with forever. Economists call this an *equilibrium*, a type of balance or state of affairs which, in this case, is impossible to improve upon by doing a little less of one thing and a little more of another.

Defined this way, every person–and every business, government agency, social club, or other decision making entity–has its own equilibrium, its own arrangement of assets and activities beyond which further improvement is impossible. Whether we are rich or poor, of modest or abundant aptitudes, this optimum level of satisfaction is what all our decision behavior is shooting for. Indeed, much economic and management theory is premised on the quest for and existence of such definable and realizable equilibria.

How dismaying, then, to learn that such equilibria don't exist. The problem isn't that they can't be calculated; economists have created marvelously complex theories and computer driven models calculating such equilibria. The problem, for one, is that these equilibria are perceived in the minds of people, and people constantly change their minds. When we tell ourselves, "I can't think of anything better to do," it's not always an expression of being optimally satisfied with the current arrangement of our affairs. It may be quite the opposite, a signal of dissatisfaction, an indication that soon something is about to give.

For another, equilibria are created by juggling combinations of real assets, and real assets–especially when they are intensely used– change, deteriorate, and wear out. This latter effect is the economic manifestation of the Second Law of Thermodynamics, the so-called entropy law. What this law decrees, in this case, is a kind of "Catch 22." That is, the very process of approaching an equilibrium tends to destroy the basis on which it was calculated. For example, by the time we have slept enough, eaten enough, worked and played enough, and done all of the other things we want and need to do enough of in a day, so that we have come close to an equilibrium of all the day's activities, we will probably be so tuckered out that we will be ready to go to bed again. A perfect equilibrium, it seems, can be an ever-receding horizon.

Even more important–and dealt with in Chapter 11–in the process of pursuing an equilibrium, we tend to change the world around us permanently. This means that the originally envisioned equilibrium may no longer be desirable and may not even be applicable. This may not be especially noticeable on the level of individual decision making, because, as individuals, we may have little perceivable impact on our environment. But taken together as a whole society and economy, we must realize that all our individual activities as producers and consumers have an enormous impact on our environment. Ozone holes, urban congestion, aquifer depletions, the exhaustion of our petroleum reserves, and so on–all resulting from the avid pursuit of optimal equilibria–inevitably change the definition of optimal equilibria themselves. Nothing holds still. Life, it seems, even business life and economic life, is always dynamic.

Thinking Like an Economist

So, we may ask, what's the point of this chapter. Indeed, what's the point of this whole book so far? If equilibria don't exist–except, perhaps, as fleeting coincidences in real life or as imaginary constructs in economic theoreticians' computers–why go through this whole cumbersome analysis of a myriad of marginal values?

There are two answers, either one of which would suffice. First of all, aspiring to unachievable goals is common and perfectly normal behavior. By definition, the only goals that can exist in the long run are unachievable, because goals that have been achieved cease to exist as goals. Complete happiness, success, love, adventure, beauty, security, religious salvation, and most of our other important goals tend to be incompletely achievable or, at least, very fragile. If they could be nailed down pat, as an accomplished and permanent fact, they would cease to give our lives direction. So, it would seem that an unachievable optimum economic equilibrium is in good company.

Secondly and finally, there is no other basis for rational behavior than that being described here. It (speaking rationally, of course) simply makes sense to gather as much data as we can, assign values or subjective utilities (both positive and negative) to our options, make decisions at the margin, and to proceed incrementally. Simply put, this is the economic way of thinking.

Attempts to find other explanations for rational behavior are always being made. Everything from genetic codes to class conflict to supernatural powers have been suggested, and some of these may, indeed, exert some influence. But rational, economic, businesslike behavior requires weighing and comparing available alternatives, and estimating values that are subject to the law of eventually diminishing marginal returns. All of this takes place in a dynamic reality, in which information is incomplete and often continues to flow, and in which our perceptions are changeable. It's always a tall order, and it's often a mess, but it's the only way we can get the most bang for the buck.

Chapter 4

BUSINESS SUCCESS

> *It is only for the sake of profit that any man employs a capital in the support of industry; and he will always, therefore, endeavor to employ it in the support of that industry of which the produce is likely to be of the greatest value.*
>
> —Adam Smith (1723-1790), Scottish political economist

If decision making is actually less complicated for businesses, it's because businesses can estimate their costs and benefits, and measure their successes or their failures, in terms of money.

The Bottom Line

The measurement of successes and failures in monetary terms is both good news and bad news. The good news is that, instead of estimating and comparing vague utilities and satisfactions with one another, everything boils down to dollars and cents. As a result, the factors that go into decisions can be seen with much clearer resolution, and decision outcomes can be much more accurately gauged. The hard discipline of money takes the fuzzies out of economic thinking.

The bad news is that, in this narrow focus on money, other values can become lost and forgotten. To be sure, decent businesses concern themselves with moral issues and environmental and social responsibilities. They take pride in a good product honestly produced. But the hard discipline of money can also blind us to the important nonmonetary values in our lives, sometimes leaving us much reduced in human stature and well-being. Nevertheless, the bottom line for businesses, so to speak, is the bottom line. They must make money. Businesses that don't succeed in this regard don't survive to concern themselves about anything else.

Except for this, business decisions operate along the same logic as other economic decisions. This can best be shown by some simple monetary examples that tell a story very much like the story told by the numerical examples in Chapter 3, examples and logic that make use of marginal analysis, which is one of the most important tools in the economist's tool kit.

Optimizing With Marginal Analysis

Suppose that a hypothetical business has ten dollars to spend on advertising this month. (We're not talking about a major corporation here.) Let's say it could print up and display posters at one dollar each, or it could give away free samples, also at one dollar per sample. The business's market research department estimates that both these tactics will generate extra, but marginally diminishing, sales revenues. Estimates of these marginal revenues generated by each dollar of advertising are given in the tables below. Again, please bear with these numerical examples. They are very simple.

Dollar spent on posters:	1	2	3	4	5	6	7	8	9	10
Resulting marginal revenue, in dollars:	12	11	10	10	9	9	8	8	8	7
Dollar spent on free samples:	1	2	3	4	5	6	7	8	9	10
Resulting marginal revenue, in dollars:	10	10	10	9	9	8	8	8	7	6

Ten dollars spent on posters are estimated to generate a total of 92 extra dollars in sales revenues; ten dollars spent on free samples only generate 85 extra dollars. But, would a mix of posters and free samples created by spending each successive advertising dollar on either a poster or a free sample, whichever would bring the most extra sales revenue–that is allocations based on marginal analysis–be any better? Let's examine this proposition in the same manner we examined the sleep/awake decisions of the last chapter.

To do so, we would start where the marginal revenue per dollar spent is the highest, which would be on posters, or "P" for short. After spending four dollars in this manner, marginal revenue would drop to $9, unless a switch is made to issuing free samples, designated by the "S" in the illustration below. The pattern would continue until the advertising budget is exhausted, but now the firm has acquired a total of $100 dollars of additional revenue, which is better than either of the two advertising strategies by themselves:

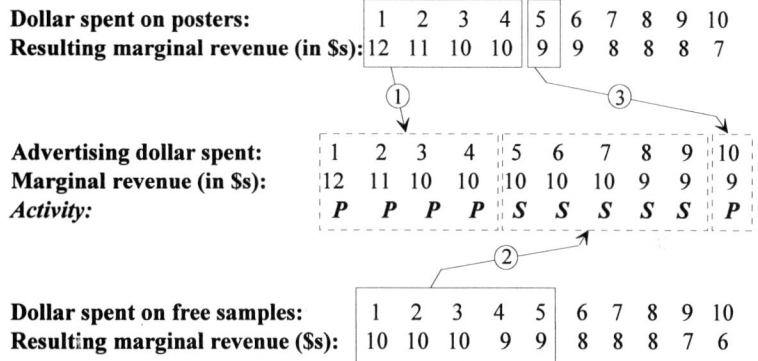

Note that the mix of dollars spent on posters and dollars spent on free samples is optimized (produces the largest amount of extra sales revenues) at the combination where the marginal revenues of each per dollar spent are equal to another. In this example, that occurs at five posters and five free samples, where the marginal revenue is nine dollars per extra dollar spent. Other combinations of posters and free samples are possible, of course, *but none will result in higher additional revenues.*

This recognition becomes a general rule. The best way to allocate dollars among alternative costs in business, as in all of life's endeavors, is to spend them so that all the alternatives' estimated marginal revenues per dollar are equal. Otherwise, total revenues could be improved by spending a little less on one alternative and a little more on another.

Obviously advertising really paid off in our little example above, and because of that the firm might want to give some thought to expanding the modest $10 budget. However, just how much expansion depends on a number of things, including the marginal cost of advertising. After all, if the firm expands its efforts in this area, it would eventually have to turn to increasingly expensive media such as newsprint, radio, and, in due time, television, where a unit of advertising may cost substantially more than a dollar for a poster or a free sample. In other words, the marginal cost of advertising is expected to go up at some point.

The "Golden Rule"

Fortunately, there is a simple way to find the level of advertising that will maximize profits whenever revenues and costs are both changing–it's where the marginal cost (MC) of advertising the last unit of output is equal to the marginal revenue (MR) derived from the sale of that same last unit of output. The equality of MR and MC, often expressed as MR = MC, is the "golden rule" of profit maximization.

To see why this is so, look at the figure on the next page which shows MC increasing as production increases (shown as a movement from left to right along the horizontal axis). Unlike the diagrams on page 9 in Chapter 2, only the tops of the unit columns are indicated, and, since there are so many units, the tops run together in uninterrupted lines. This increase in marginal cost occurs because the business is likely to use the *least* costly sources of inputs first–its cheapest or most cost-efficient labor, its lowest-cost materials, its most efficient factories–and then move on to more expensive ones as the lower cost opportunities are exhausted. By the same token, marginal revenue, the revenue from the sale of the next unit of output, decreases as production expands (an inexorable consequence of the law of diminishing marginal returns, which tells us that prices have to be lowered to encourage consumers to buy additional quantities of a given product).

Of course, the firm never really knows the exact shape or location of the MR and MC curves (shown as straight lines here even though economists customarily speak of curves), but it doesn't need to know, as long as the firm proceeds incrementally. For example, when the firm produces its 100th unit, it discovers that the MR from the sale of that unit ($8) is greater than the MC of producing that unit ($4). The difference between the two, $4, is profit, and so the business is tempted to expand production to obtain more profits.

When the firm produces its 200th unit, it finds that the MR from the sale ($7) is still greater than the MC of production ($5), leaving $2 profit on the unit. As long as the marginal cost of producing the next unit of output is less than the marginal revenue from the sale of that unit, additional units will be produced.

Eventually, however, a point is reached where MR is *equal* to MC, leaving the firm with no profit on this unit of output. In fact, the firm finds this level of output more or less by trial and error. If it makes a profit (however small) on the 298th unit, it will be encouraged to produce the 299th unit. And, if this is profitable, it will try to produce and sell the 300th unit. At this level, however, MR is equal to MC and therefore no additional profits will be secured. With no additional profits, there will be no incentive to produce the 301st unit.

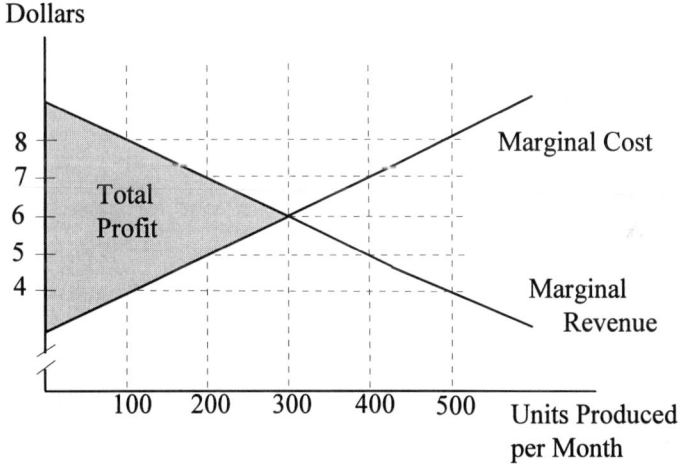

In other words, if the firm ceases to add to its total profits when MC is equal to MR, then the equality of MR=MC must indicate the level of production that maximizes profits.

If we look back at our diagram, it should also be evident that the *total profits* from production is equal to the shaded area where MR is greater than MC. This is true because the shaded area is the sum of the $8 profit from the 100th unit, the $4 profit from the sale of the 200th unit, and all of the other profits from the sale of other units ranging from 1 to 300.

Finally, this general rule can be carried to an even grander logical conclusion. For factors of production that can't be broken down to single dollar amounts, as in the case where we can't buy a single dollar's worth of a bulldozer or a computer, we have:

$$\frac{MR_A}{MC_A} = \frac{MR_B}{MC_B} = \ldots = \frac{MR_N}{MC_N} = 1,$$

where subscripts A through N designate the marginal revenues and costs associated with the *last* unit of the different factors of production (the bulldozer or the computer) purchased, or even different activities such as the advertising example above.

When this logical conclusion is reached, not only are the dollar costs of production being allocated optimally among all the factors of production, the optimum total number of dollars is being spent on this entire business venture. Spend less than this, so that

$$\frac{MR_N}{MC_N} > 1,$$

and the business is *under*shooting its profit maximizing optimum. (Be reminded that, true to the law of eventually diminishing marginal returns–see page 9–the *more* we make use of something, the *less* returns will be yielded by the last incremental unit of that something. That is why marginal revenue goes down when we expand production, or up when we contract it.)

Or, in terms of the figure on the previous page, marginal revenue can only be greater than marginal cost when the firm is producing fewer than 300 units of output–which means that the firm is shy of producing at the rate of output that maximizes profits. By the same logic, it can also be seen that in cases where marginal cost is greater than marginal revenue (at levels of production greater than 300), losses will be incurred which reduce total profits. Once again, only when

$$\frac{MR_N}{MC_N} = 1,$$

is the optimum achieved.

All of which seems frightfully precise and mathematical. In actual fact, it rarely is. The marginal revenues and marginal costs are all estimates, so calculating them right down to the penny is pretty difficult, if not impossible. Even if we could calculate them, they wouldn't be established facts, because they haven't happened yet. That is, they are the estimates on which business' decisions to do something–to advertise some more, or to buy another bulldozer, whatever–are based.

Surely most of these estimates, like all predictions in real life, will prove to be a little inaccurate and will require further decisions, not only to straighten them out, but also to take into account new circumstances and new opportunities that always seem to crop up. In the meantime, the process never stops. There is no relief from having to make business (or any other kind of) decisions–which is why it always pays to have a strategy of proceeding incrementally in the face of uncertainty.

Thinking Like an Economist

Perhaps only economics books explain the logic of marginal analysis and only economists advocate it. But most, if not all, rational business decisions follow the processes of marginal analyses, whether the decision makers know it or not. This is the process that is being addressed when decision makers ask those most fundamental of all business questions, "Is it worthwhile? Will it pay for itself?"

Marginal decision making by no means guarantees the success of the business or the individual in the market. Excellently managed businesses may fail, and badly mismanaged businesses may succeed, because the markets in which they compete don't really care about how well businesses are managed. However, it can be argued that marginal decision making is the best strategy to employ, if the intended outcome is to secure positive profits–and without these profits, survival is not assured. More will be said about this in the next chapter.

Notice, by the way, that, in all the preceding marginal analysis and especially in the numerical advertising examples, we assumed that the costs per month or whatever accounting period the firm is using could be easily increased or decreased, that they are what economists call *variable costs*. In fact, many important costs, such as the costs of plant and equipment, are relatively fixed. Deciding on the best amounts of these costs can become more like heroic and less like marginal decisions, but nobody said that running a business is easy.

In the end, in business, the proof of the pudding is in the actual dollars and cents results. If the firm proceeds incrementally (so that bad decisions can be reversed), and if estimated marginal revenues and marginal costs are reasonably accurate, total revenues from sales should be maximized successfully.

Chapter 5

PRICES AND MARKETS

> *The great advantage of the market . . . is that it permits wide diversity. It is, in political terms, a system of proportional representation. Each man can vote, as it were, for the color of tie he wants and get it; he does not have to see what color the majority wants and then, if he is in the minority, submit.*
>
> – Milton Friedman (1912-), American Nobel Prize winning economist

Markets are one of the more remarkable structures of our time. Technically, markets exist wherever people (or businesses) get together to exchange products. Some markets–ranging from tiny flea markets to much bigger organizations such as the New York Stock Exchange–exist in distinct physical locations. Others, such as the NASDAQ Over-The-Counter market, exist in cyberspace. Markets are ubiquitous, and we would have a hard time living without them.

A Win-Win Situation

First and foremost, markets allow us to be better off because they (at least in the ideal envisioned by the economist) are voluntary. What matters in markets is that sellers can sell and that buyers can buy at prices that both find acceptable. When a price is found that satisfies these conditions for both sellers and buyers, everyone becomes better off as a result of every sale and purchase.

This is an important point. Buyers and sellers need each other! When they agree on a price, both go away better off–or, at least, not worse off–than they were before. This is true by definition: since buying and selling are voluntary acts, neither party would agree to participate, if they estimated that they would be worse off after the exchange than they were before. To be sure, one participant often gets more out of a deal than the other, which makes it seem that market exchange is an "I-win-you-lose" game between the participants, like baseball. It is not. (And actually, baseball is not an entirely I-win-you-lose game either. If it were, no team would agree to play unless it had a reasonable probability of a win for itself.)

Moreover, the competition found in markets isn't just between the buyer and seller; sellers compete with each other for customers, and buyers compete with one another to get the best price from sellers. This makes markets the most efficient and economically logical way of publicly allocating goods and services from producers to consumers ever devised. Neither the bureaucratically controlled systems of communism or other dictatorships, nor the social custom-controlled systems of primitive tribes and peasant societies, have turned out to be up to the task. Especially in recent years, we have seen one economy after another abandon its nonmarket allocation system and switch to a market system instead.

Prices As Signals

Most markets, such as shopping malls, stock exchanges, city downtowns, and so on, consist of more than one buyer and more than one seller, each with his and her own set of preferences and eagernesses to buy and sell. To the degree that markets are public and price information is openly available to all, no one will pay a higher price or accept a lower price than necessary, even if their personal eagernesses would allow them to do so.

The result is that market prices tend to concentrate around one price for all the buyers and sellers of a particular kind of commodity. And, in each case, these single prices represent the highest price that the least eager buyer in the market will pay and the lowest price that the least eager seller in the market will accept. Those who are more eager get especially good bargains, and those who won't or can't buy or sell at the market price won't buy or sell at all.

Collectively, participants in markets work to establish uniform (or fairly uniform, depending on the market) prices. Economists often think of these prices in terms of "signals" that influence behavior. High prices serve to discourage consumers and encourage producers. Low prices have the opposite effect of encouraging consumers and discouraging producers. It seems almost paradoxical: markets are made up of groups (buyers and sellers) whose interests are diametrically opposed to one another–and yet the more competitive the market, the more efficient the outcome and the more uniform the prevailing price.

Supply and Demand

Economists have developed a very neat way of describing this process via what they call supply and demand analysis. First, all potential buyers of a specific product and all the potential sellers of that product are lumped together as demanders and suppliers respectively. These two groups form the market, which can be local, such as the market for haircuts, or national–even international–such as the market for soybeans; it can be small, such as the market for clarinet reeds, or large, such as the market for gasoline.

All market activity–that is, all buying and selling–is perceived as occurring over some conveniently chosen time period, such as per day, or per month, or even per year. Also, economists prefer to define a separate market for each specific kind of product, such as the residential electricity use market or the market for unsalted Grade A butter (although, in real life, many kinds of goods may be bought and sold in a single supermarket, department store, or catalogue).

If all of this sounds a little abstract or hypothetical, be assured that it is! Of course, demanders, suppliers, and the resulting markets do actually exist. But the price of economic analysis here and in many other applications is to extract an imaginary construct from reality. Only in this way can complex reality be simplified enough to submit to effective analysis. Much of what follows is such an abstraction, but one which actually contributes to our understanding.

We start with demanders in a market who may be (and probably are) perfect strangers to one another. Except in special situations, some of them mentioned later in chapter, they act as independent individuals. And they include customers who are willing and able to pay high prices for the market's product, as well as those who are willing or able only to pay a low price. But, of course, given the opportunity, all of the demanders would rather pay a low price, assuming that the quality and everything else about the product stays the same. Naturally, then, there will be more of the product demanded at low prices than at high prices, as show in the hypothetical chart below.

Price of the product: $1.10 1.20 1.30 1.40 1.50
Total quantity demanded by all demanders: 2,100 1,800 1,500 1,200 900

This inverse relationship between price and quantity is called the "Law of Demand." For reasons that will soon become apparent, economists like to present this data graphically, as in the diagram shown here:

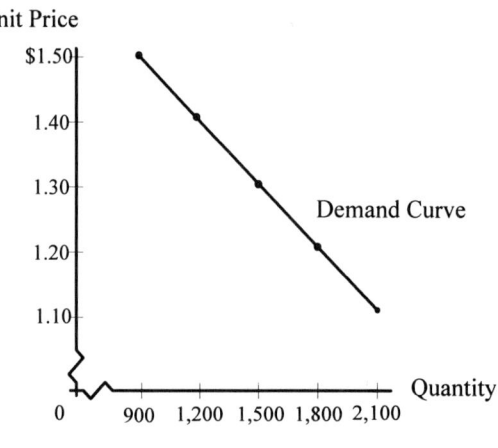

Prospective sellers of the product are also assumed to act individually in the competitive market process, except in special situations, some of which will also be dealt with later in the chapter. Like demanders, suppliers include the eager and able, as well as the reluctant or less able. But, given the opportunity, all of them would prefer to supply the product at a high price, and less of the product will be supplied at lower prices. (A word of caution here: don't be fooled by the fact that many products are "cheaper by the dozen" and sold at quantity discounts. When this occurs, the product itself changes. A six-pack of twelve-ounce cans in the grocery store is a very different product from a refrigerated and conveniently available can in a vending machine, even if it is the same brand. As such, they exist in separate markets.) This direct relationship between price and quantity is called the "Law of Supply," and is illustrated by the relationships in the following chart:

Price of the product:	$1.10	1.20	1.30	1.40	1.50
Total quantity offered by all suppliers:	900	1,200	1,500	1,800	2,100

The law of supply, like the law of demand, can be represented in the form of a graph. If we calibrate the axes exactly as we did for the demand curve above, and then plot the price-quantity pairings, our graph looks like the one shown here. The upward-sloping function is a way of visualizing the assumption that sellers would be willing to offer more products at higher prices and less at lower ones.

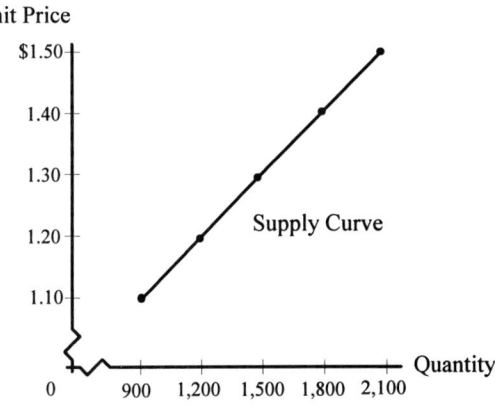

Supply and demand represent the two sides, so to speak, of the same market. And, because we have taken care to illustrate the law of demand and the law of supply using diagrams which are calibrated exactly alike, we can now superimpose them to form the single most famous (infamous?) diagram in economics, shown below.

A glance shows that, at a price of $1.30, the eagerness of demanders to buy equals the eagerness of the supplier to sell; or, the quantity demanded, 1500 units, equals the quantity supplied. Economists celebrate this confluence by calling it a market equilibrium, referring to the price and quantity as the equilibrium price and the equilibrium quantity. The intersection of the demand and supply "curves" (shown here as

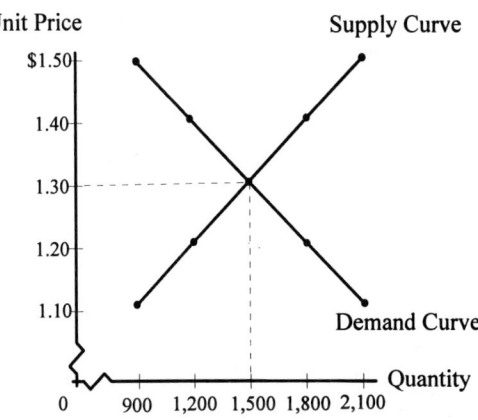

straight lines) indicates more clearly than anything else the equilibrium price and quantity in that market.

But be reminded, even if the real market prices and quantities happen to coincide with the equilibrium prices and quantities in these schedules, the rest of the numbers do not come from real experience. They are, at best, the carefully researched estimates of the market. At worst, they are simply "guesstimates" off the top of somebody's head. Given the often erratic nature of consumer and producer preferences, the accuracy of these estimates is never guaranteed.

Market Dynamics

The economist's models of supply and demand are marvelous explanatory devices for the market process. For example, in the above case, if we assume that the price of the product moves up to $1.40, demanders would presumably only want to buy 1,200 of them, while suppliers are estimated to want to offer 1,800 of them for sale. The 600 unsold products sitting on the shelves would only be sold if their price would be lowered again, simultaneously signaling suppliers to reduce the quantity supplied and demanders to increase the quantity demanded.

Conversely, if the price were to be too low, let's say $1.20, the estimated 1,800 products demanded will far exceed the 1,200 supplied. The shortage would drive up the price, which would signal suppliers to increase the quantity of the product supplied and demanders to decrease the quantity demanded.

And so, through the signals given by price movements, markets are seen as self-correcting. A market clearing price, at which the quantities supplied equal the quantities demanded–in other words, an equilibrium price–is the ultimate goal. For many markets, such as for stocks and many agricultural goods, prices can change virtually every minute. In other markets, the butcher shops and green grocers in our supermarkets, prices change only every several days. For relatively durable brand name products, such as tennis rackets or personal computers, prices can be fixed for weeks or months. But eventually, if the quantity demanded outruns the quantity supplied, even penny candy will cost a nickel; and if the quantity supplied exceeds the quantity demanded, even fancy $100 running shoes can be had for $39.95.

Perfect competition–the ideal market situation that features many buyers and sellers, products that are virtually indistinguishable from one another, ease of entry into (and exit from) the market, and readily available and accurate information about prices–tends to generate market prices that are about as low as it is technically possible for them to be. Sellers who might want to raise prices even a little are pushed out of the market by sellers who can live with the lower market price. As a further result, this lowest technically possible market price allows the most customers possible to participate in the market. So perfect competition guarantees the most goods for the most people at the lowest possible price.

Imperfect Markets

But, conditions for perfect competition seldom exist. Instead, most businesses in modern economies produce products that are carefully differentiated from other similar products by their designs, by their trademarks, by their patents and copyrights, and by their advertising claiming distinction and superiority. Many major industries have only a few–think of a dozen or two–sellers. Information is often jealously guarded, and newcomers are not made welcome. All of this is the stuff from which serious business competition is made, and economists, forever eager to make order out of complex reality, distinguish three major categories of such imperfect competition.

Monopolistic competition is the most common category. The name is misleading, because these firms are hardly large, rapacious monopolies. Instead, they are the many small businesses–beauty salons, corner pubs, print shops, building contractors, and so on–whose products are differentiated from one another by virtue of their location, their service, and/or their uniqueness. These firms don't have good access to information, and they tend to come and go with alarming rapidity. But, hope blooms eternal, so there are always plenty of monopolistic competitors ready to have a go at success.

It's quite another story with *oligopolies* (from the Greek *oligo* - few, and *poly* - sellers). Here we have typical corporate America: the automobile manufacturers, home appliance producers, soap companies, and so forth. Their products may be either differentiated (automobiles) or homogeneous (steel), but the distinguishing characteristic is that they are big players in their markets. They tend to have powerful influences on each other, so they jockey for market dominance. And, like good poker players, they guard their information jealously. Newcomers can only muscle into oligopolistic markets with great difficulty.

Finally, there are *monopolies*, single sellers by definition–if not always in reality–who have their entire markets to themselves, so they need not share any information or distinguish their products at all. The various public utilities, such as water, gas, and electricity, fall into this category and are often called *natural monopolies*, because it seems natural to have only one seller in such markets. Competition would require more than one seller and, in the case of public utilities, would require wasteful duplication of transmission lines and pipelines. In such cases, government agencies–usually called "public utilities commissions"–are empowered to ride herd on the prices and products supplied by the utilities.

To be sure, some minor market imperfections and monopolistic tactics aren't all bad. Larger firms are often able to take advantage of the more efficient economies of large scale production, and higher profits encourage investments in research and development. Furthermore, differentiated products make shopping a lot more fun for customers. Recognizing this, governments establish exclusive patents and copyrights for the production of some goods and services (including this book). Advertising and product design intentionally present some products as unique and irreplaceable. Finally, we don't have much choice. Requiring a typical American corporation, let's say General Electric, to become a perfect competitor would be like requiring an ocean liner to become a canoe. Not very realistic.

However, imperfect competitors often present worrisome opportunities for mischief. The more the buyers are convinced that they cannot get along without a particular product, that there are no real substitutes for it, and that they would pay almost any price for it, the more monopolistic power the supplier will enjoy. The price can be jacked up without losing very many sales, and profits can soar. Being the exclusive seller of addictive drugs in your neighborhood is an extreme–but illegal–example of such monopoly powers, but it goes far to explain why drug pushers often kill each other to defend their turf. The large and small sellers of legal products, from auto supply stores to zipper companies, desire the same monopoly powers, although thankfully, in a milder way. They want to tie their customers exclusively to themselves.

Economists say that customers in such a fix have relatively *inelastic* demands for these products, because they have few alternatives, are unable or unwilling to delay the purchase, and are willing to pay higher prices. Sellers, too, can be in such a fix. They can find themselves with a product line that is their only business activity. They must sell it almost at any price. Appropriately, economists say that suppliers in such a fix have relatively inelastic supplies. In business, as in life, it is best to avoid being in such inelastic straits. Having many alternatives ready and available at all times–having elastic demands or elastic supplies–if we can arrange it, is the best situation possible.

We should note that this logic can be extended to situations such as those involving contacts with others–relationships which can be profitable if they have an inelastic relationship with us. If others can be made to believe that they can deal with no one but us, we could always negotiate the best possible deals for ourselves and we could always get the most favorable prices, leading to the most profits and least costs, both in monetary and nonmonetary terms. This is well understood by the fatally attractive women and men among us. It is no less well understood by the economically sophisticated.

Thinking Like an Economist

Economists are not so naive as to believe that all allocations take place within the framework of supply and demand. In almost all economies of whatever stripe, the last few steps of product allocation–getting goods and services to the final consumers–usually do not involve a market. For example, there is not much buying or selling within the family. Parents may pay their kids for mowing the lawn or washing the dishes, but parents provide the basic food, clothing, and shelter free of charge. This nonmarket allocation within families and other close-knit groups is difficult to analyze because interpersonal comparisons of value are difficult to make. We may know very clearly that we prefer a dish of ice cream to the price we have to pay for it, thus justifying its purchase. But we don't know this nearly as clearly when we buy it for our children or for a close friend.

Indeed, the further removed people are from each other, the more difficult interpersonal comparisons of value become. We may think we know the various preferences of our spouses and children reasonably well, but friends become more of a mystery and strangers may as well live on another planet. Yet, much of our public policy is premised on the belief that we can generally predict what the mass of people will want and how badly they want it. The basis for this belief is that it makes sense to assume that a dollar means more to a pauper than to a millionaire. So one intention of "progressive" tax policies and social welfare programs is to reallocate money and resources from those that have to those that have not. It is a difficult mission. Anyone who has tried to share things equitably, even among close family members, knows that justice in the nonmarket distribution of goods and services is an elusive and evanescent quantity.

The beauty of market justice is that it is more obvious. The more eagerly people want to buy a commodity, the more they will pay for it. And the more eagerly people want to sell a commodity, the lower the price will be that they accept for it. People may appear to make decisions for a number of reasons, but the economist would argue that people make decisions incrementally; that they weigh the inevitable calculus of opportunity costs and benefits of their actions (at times subjectively); and that the long arm of the law of diminishing marginal returns is at work throughout. Markets not only make these decisions possible, they make them more efficient.

Chapter 6

THE GAINS FROM TRADE

> *Commerce is the grand panacea, which, like a beneficent medical discovery, will serve to inoculate with the healthy and saving taste for civilization all the nations of the world.*
>
> *– Robert Cobden (1804-1865), English economist and statesman*

Markets that function well provide the most goods and services at the lowest possible prices to the most customers and make both buyers and sellers better off than they were before. This, after all, is the only reason for markets to exist and the only reason we return to them again and again in our daily lives. In fact, no other economic system is able to get as many goods and services out to as many people as effectively as can a market economy.

The Grand Panacea

It comes somewhat of a surprise, therefore, to find that many of those who accept free market economics at home are suspicious of international trade. Buying and selling among ourselves may be perfectly OK, but "watch out for those foreigners!" Yet, the only thing that distinguishes international trade from doing business here at home is that it involves crossing international boundaries and usually involves exchanging currencies. Otherwise, the fundamentals are the same: it is a voluntary coming together of buyers and sellers, who both expect to be made better off by the trade.

A simple arithmetic that economists call the "Theory of Comparative Advantage" illustrates this very well. Again, follow along with this numerical explanation. It is very simple.

The Law of Comparative Advantage

Suppose we have two countries, the USA and the ROW (Rest Of the World) that both produce, let's say, woolen cloth and wine. The table below shows the total production–measured in barrels of wine and bolts of wool–that could be produced in each country in one day's time:

	Total Production in One Day: in the USA	in the ROW
Barrels of Wine	10	4
Bolts of Wool	5	4

Notice that in this hypothetical example the United States can produce more of both products on any given day than can the ROW. So obviously, the USA has nothing to gain from trade, right?

Wrong!

A closer look reveals that the USA can produce 2 barrels of wine for every bolt of wool (10 wine/5 wool), while the ROW can only produce 1 barrel of wine for every bolt of wool (4 wine/4 wool). A clever American trader with 10 barrels of wine would be smart to take the wine to the ROW and exchange it for 10 bolts of wool (where 1 barrel of wine = 1 bolt of wool), instead of exchanging it for only 5 bolts of wool at home. Then, the trader could bring the wool back to the USA and exchange it for 20 barrels of wine (where 2 barrels of wine = 1 bolt of wool)–leaving a profit of 10 barrels of wine for the venture. Assuming, for the sake of simplicity, that there are no shipping, management, transactions, or capital costs, this comes to a tidy 100 percent profit on just one exchange! A person could get rich on just a few of these trades.

A trader in the ROW could play the same game. If the trader starts out with wool, he or she would be better off selling it in the USA where every bolt of wool exchanges for 2 barrels of wine. So, the trader would take 4 bolts of wool to the USA, exchange them for 8 barrels of wine, and then bring the wine back to the ROW. Once home, the 8 barrels of wine would be exchanged for 8 bolts of wool given the 1-to-1 exchange ratio. Again, a beginning investment of 4 wool could be turned into 8 wool in the absence of transportation and other charges. And, just like the American trader, the ROW trader realizes the same 100 percent profit on the round trip.

Eventually, people in the USA will discover that wine is in demand, and so they will produce more of it and less wool (which they can import from the ROW). Likewise, people in the ROW will find that their wool is in demand–causing them to produce more wool and less wine (which they can import from the USA). The result is that both countries begin to specialize in the good in which they have a *comparative advantage*. A country (or even an individual for that matter) has a comparative advantage in the production of a product when it can produce that product relatively more efficiently, or at a lower opportunity cost, than can another. In this example, the USA has a comparative advantage in the production of wine, while the ROW has a comparative advantage in the production of wool.

The Welfare Effects of Trade

As both countries begin to specialize along the lines of their comparative advantage, something remarkable happens–both countries experience an increase in total welfare! After all, if each country produces the product that they can produce relatively more efficiently, then more products will be produced overall, and everyone in both countries is theoretically better off! We say theoretically, because we cannot be sure of the distribution of the benefits in each country.

Admittedly, simple arithmetic examples such as this can hardly deal with the full dynamics of a real trading situation. First of all, many more than just two kinds of commodities are traded. And then, the trading business itself is likely to have an impact on the efficiency with which products are produced, changing the original exchange ratios. Furthermore, there will be some shipping, transactions, and management costs. Also, welfare gains from trade–like many other things in life such as health, beauty, and intelligence–may not be distributed evenly among all citizens. Some individuals or groups may get more than others, and some may get nothing extra at all, but this is a matter of income distribution which, while important, does not negate the overall increase in welfare due to trade.

But the essential logic remains! As long as the domestic production ratios (wine for wool in the example used here) for each country are not identical, international trade will be a profitable opportunity. Furthermore, that one country produces less or more of a product than another doesn't really matter. Test this out by multiplying ROW's 4 wine and 4 wool in the table by 100, turning these numbers into 400 and 400 respectively. This does not change the production ratios in either country, but it does make the ROW a very productive region indeed. Next, rework the example starting with an American trader selling 10 barrels of wine in the ROW. Amazingly, the trade will proceed and be just as profitable as before!

This reveals a crucial point and exposes a popular misconception about trade: that a country is better off when it produces *absolutely* more of a product (whether it be wine or wool) than other countries. This is not the engine of trade. Instead, what drives trade is that some country can produce a product *relatively more efficiently* than can other countries.

Since this analysis applies to people as well as to countries–we could just as well change the labels USA and ROW to read Bob and Alice–it becomes, perhaps, the most benign, well-meaning, and welcome law in all of economics. It explains, in the irrefutable logic of its simple arithmetic, why all of us, rich or poor, strong or weak, smart or dull, energetic or lazy, can gain from trade with any or all the rest of us. The only two people who have nothing to offer each other would be those who have exactly identical productivity ratios within themselves. No two people like that have ever been found.

There is one last, and very important, thing we should keep in mind–the parallel that exists between individuals that trade and nations that trade. Recall, from the last chapter, that individuals trade only because both are better off after trade than before the trade took place. Nations trade for the same reasons. Once a price is agreed upon, and as long as buying and selling are voluntary acts, neither party would agree to participate unless they believed that they would be better off after the exchange than they were before the trade took place. In this regard, trade between nations is an extension of trade between individuals, and it opens new opportunities for gain that would not otherwise be possible.

Opposition to Trade

So, then, why do some people or groups oppose trade so vehemently? Why do auto workers sometime stone foreign-made automobiles? Why do Indiana corn-broom makers oppose NAFTA? Why do textile towns fear trade with Asia? Why do sugar farmers oppose free international markets for their products? Some might argue that ignorance is one reason, or that the nuances of comparative advantage are so subtle and intricate as to defy understanding by large numbers of people. But, that's not it. We could argue that people are simply xenophobic–that their fear of foreigners simply overwhelms their rational desire to become better off through the positive welfare effects of trade. But, that's not it either.

Instead, those who oppose trade are usually acting in an entirely rational and incremental manner, carefully balancing their own personal costs against their own personal benefits to arrive at a perfectly logical conclusion.

The reason for this is that the benefits of trade are thinly spread throughout the economy. We have a broader choice of cars (not to mention lower prices) because of the competition provided by foreign car makers. Corn brooms from Mexico are cheaper than those made in Indiana, giving consumers alternative products, and lower priced ones at that, from which to choose. Inexpensive fabrics and clothing from the Pacific rim provide additional low-cost alternatives for consumers. Domestic sugar producers, by contrast, have so far been successful in restricting our international trade in sugar, and so have denied consumers the benefits of lower sugar costs in this country.

In short, the opposition to freer trade stems from the fact that those who are threatened by trade–auto producers, corn broom producers, textile producers, sugar producers–suffer intensely when trade actually materializes, often costing people their jobs, their industries, and even their communities. In fact, the costs are often so great that they can get the attention of a sympathetic senator or representative who is willing to "take action" to save an endangered way of life. Worse, these representatives are often willing to trade their support with others in Congress who are doing exactly the same thing for producers of other threatened products in their states.

What about the opinions from those of us who have nothing in particular to lose from trade, and yet benefit incrementally every time the variety of competitively priced goods and services available to us increases? Surprisingly, the answer is that we normally do little, if anything, to counter those groups who oppose freer trade.

This too is a perfectly rational decision based on incremental evaluations of personal cost-benefit analysis. After all, the annual benefits of lower corn broom or sugar prices are likely to be so small as to be difficult to measure–providing that we even know about them in the first place. The benefits of having more higher quality and lower price choices among clothing and automobiles is a bit more obvious, but it's still difficult for those who benefit from trade to organize effectively against each and every one of the lobbyist groups that push anti-trade legislation.

As a result, national trade policy is (potentially) affected by two main groups. On one side, we have a very large group of average consumers who, because of the cost-benefit calculus, have little incentive to organize politically to thwart those who oppose freer trade. On the other side, we have a very small group of intense and vocal trade opponents who, by their own cost-benefit calculations, have every reason to protect certain products or industries.

The irony in all this is that protectionists are usually all too willing to enjoy the benefits of trade when it suits them, and to oppose it when it does not. Indiana corn broom makers are all too willing to wear clothing made in Asia, shoes made in South America, and (perhaps to a lesser extent) drive cars made abroad. Likewise, people in American textile industry towns buy Mexican brooms, foreign cars, and other products from abroad because they like the variety, quality, or simply the price.

Foreign Currency Exchange Rates

Even if we wouldn't dream of ever setting foot outside the good old USA, and even if we wouldn't buy a foreign-made product if it were the last item on the shelf, international exchange rates are important to us. These exchange rates–how many German marks, French francs, Japanese yen, or whatever foreign currency units exchange for one U.S. dollar–ride herd on America's economic relationship with the rest of the world. Fluctuations in these exchange rates can cost us lost jobs or can create new ones. They will influence our real estate and stock market prices; and they can even push up our inflation at home or keep it down.

Of course, if all the trading nations used the same kind of money, this complication wouldn't exist. Indeed, one of the great advantages of our American economy is that all fifty states use the same currency–dollars and cents–creating economic as well as political union. Trading blocks around the world, especially members of the European Union, aspire hopefully to such convenience, but so far, foreign trade today still means having to exchange currencies, one kind for the other, most of the time. If, let's say, Boeing sells airliners in France, it doesn't want to be paid in French francs. It wants U.S. dollars, because Boeing workers in Seattle want their pay in U.S. dollars. That's the only kind of money they can use at their local supermarket and all the other places they spend their paychecks. The same goes for all of Boeing's other American suppliers. But the French, of course, want to pay in francs, because that's the kind of money they earn when they sell airline tickets to their passengers.

Where are the French supposed to get U.S. dollars from, so that they can pay Boeing? The most obvious place is in America itself, where the French can sell some of their exports such as some wines and high fashion clothing. Actually, many nations use dollars for international trade, so France might also earn dollars from its exports to other nations. But, just as Boeing only wants to be paid in dollars, the French vintners and clothiers only want to be paid for their exports to America in the currency of their choice: French francs. Yet the Americans persist in paying in dollars. It's a problem.

As we can tell already, the obvious solution suggests itself: somebody ought to get the Americans and the French together to swap the currencies they *don't* want for the currencies they *do* want. This somebody is usually large banks located in major cities around the world. They are happy–for a fee–to exchange francs or almost any other of the world's currencies for dollars, and vice versa. The question still left unanswered is this: "How many francs (or other national currency units) exchange for how many dollars?" That is, what are the exchange rates between currencies, and how are these rates determined?

As we might expect by now, the answer is that the exchange rates are determined by the relative supplies of and demands for the currencies offered for exchange. If, let's say, the French buy a lot of American airliners, they will offer a lot of francs for exchange to dollars. If, at the same time, the Americans don't buy a lot of French wines and clothes, they won't be offering a lot of American dollars for exchange to francs. The predictable result will be that the abundant francs lose exchange value in relation to the scarce dollars. Fewer dollars will be needed to buy more francs or, saying the same thing the other way around, more francs will be needed to buy fewer dollars. Economists will say the franc has depreciated against the dollar, and American journalists will proclaim that the U.S. dollar has strengthened against the weakening Franc, although strength and weakness are ill chosen and irrelevant adjectives, in this context.

However, the story is not finished. If Americans could get more francs for each dollar than before, they would find all sorts of French exports becoming real bargains. Perfumes, musical instruments, weekends in Paris, etc., would become more and more affordable than before. These industries would enjoy a boom in France, and more and more U.S. dollars would be offered in exchange for francs. At the same time, and in perfect symmetry, American airliners would become more expensive and less affordable, in terms of those depreciated francs, than before. Boeing would lose some sales, and fewer francs would be offered in exchange for dollars. This new abundance of dollars and scarcity of francs would start to reverse the previous depreciation of the franc and would begin the depreciation of the dollar against the franc.

Will the exchange rate ever settle down? Those large banks in the major cities, working together with the central banks of the major trading nations, often try to manipulate the currency exchange markets to try to prevent drastic swings in exchange rates. Some nations, most notably the members of the European Union, try to hold their mutual exchange rates almost constant, in order to approximate a single currency. In any case, dealing and speculating in international currency exchanges–a job for only the most sophisticated professionals!–tends to smooth out the fluctuations. Even so, as any American tourist abroad knows, exchange rates continue to fluctuate.

The point for us to remember in all this is that exchange rates are not set by governments in most developed nations, nor are they set by some rational comparison of costs-of-living. They are set almost exclusively by the supplies of and demands for the currencies to be exchanged. And these supplies and demands are generated by the international trade that is going on. In this regard, we are simply witnessing the price system at work on global scale, where the price of one currency is stated in the number of units of another country's currency. These international prices, like the dollar prices in domestic markets, serve as signals to buyers and sellers, helping these individuals make their incremental decisions, just as we do in our local markets.

Thinking Like an Economist

Trade is driven by economic self-interest. National pride, a striving for superiority or power, the protection of special privileges, and even ideological beliefs influence international trade. But these are external to the economic motive for trade, which follows the same rationale as any other kind of market exchange: both buyers and sellers, both importers and exporters benefit from it, or, at least, are not made worse off by it. This is true by definition, because the participants in trade are acting voluntarily.

Furthermore, trade of some kind is almost universally possible, because it depends only on countries–or regions or individual people– being different from one another. And the differences that generate this trade are not necessarily the easily identifiable absolute differences, such as one country being much richer and more productive than another. Rather, what drives trade and determines its content is the dissimilarity of the comparative efficiencies of the different production processes in one country–or region or person– with the comparative efficiencies of those same production processes in another country or region or person. Since such dissimilarities are virtually guaranteed to be widespread, the potential gains from trade are also virtually guaranteed to be widespread.

This is why economists and all other people who think like economists generally champion free trade. Protectionist arguments, as logical and rational as they are to those who make them, are generally considered as being the special pleading of those who are willing to deny others the gains from trade, in order to feather their own nests or to further their own economic or even noneconomic interests. A trade restriction almost always lowers total welfare, but the cost of the restriction is borne in very small amounts by a very large number of people, while the benefits of the restriction accrue in much larger amounts to a very small number of people–all of which explains the passion and intensity exhibited by many of those who resist freer trade, and the comparative lack of intensity displayed by those who favor it.

And yet, since World War II, the world has made significant progress toward freer trade and a more interdependent global economy. These developments are a testament to the powers of the market over the vested interests of special interest groups.

Chapter 7

GOVERNMENT AND ECONOMICS

> *The ideas of economists and political philosophers, both when they are right and when they are wrong, are more powerful than is commonly understood. Indeed the world is ruled by little else. Practical men who believe themselves to be quite exempt from any intellectual influences, are usually the slaves of some defunct economist.*
>
> – John Maynard Keynes (1883-1946), English economist

About one dollar out of every three spent in America is spent by one of our federal, state, or local governments. About one dollar out of every three received as revenue is received by these governments. Today, more people in the United States work for some branch of a government than in all of manufacturing!

Collectively, government is big business. They spend enormous sums of money to operate a myriad of programs and activities. And, they need to establish a whole repertoire of laws, ordinances, and regulations–all of which powerfully impacts our daily lives. Furthermore, government in America has been a growth industry from almost the year it was founded in 1776. Regardless of the political party in power, governments tend to grow in both absolute and relative size. Consequently it is important to know why governments participate in the economy, as well as to understand the efficiency, incentives, and consequences of their decisions.

Private vs. Public Goods

The proper role of government varies, of course, according to one's point of view. However, economists view one function of government as being absolutely unambiguous–to be a provider of *public goods*, those goods and services that are collectively consumed by almost everyone, or at least a reasonably large number of people. Public goods include national defense, flood control, police protection, public highways, libraries, and a system of justice to name just a few. All these examples have one thing in common–they simply would not be available in sufficient quantities if the production of these items were left to the private sector.

The private economy does a marvelous job providing an incredible variety of goods and services–but it only produces those things that can be *withheld* if people refuse to pay for them. Someone, for example, would simply not be able to take a cruise or enjoy owning a new car, house, or other product unless they paid for them. If they were not willing to pay, these products would remain with the producer, wholesaler, retailer, or current owner until such time as they were sold. Yet, it is almost impossible to deny people the benefits of national defense, or the use of public highways, or the protection of the police and justice system, because it is so difficult to make individuals pay. Consequently the government must step in to provide a sufficient amount of public goods–and then use its power to levy taxes to recover the costs.

The need for public goods is one of the reasons that governments are such large players in an economic sense. In fact, just by itself, the federal government is the biggest single actor on the American economic stage. If we could take all our governmental units together, we would find that they make up a very substantial proportion of our entire cast of economic characters: producers, consumers, advertisers, environmentalists, international traders, landlords, regulators, and so on and on. But, they can't be taken together. Ranging from village town halls to the giant bureaucrat factory that is Washington, D.C., they are as different from one another as the corner sandwich shop is from General Motors.

Individual vs. Public Decisions

The problem is that we relate to all governments differently than we relate to private businesses and to our households. In the

Chapter 7: Government and Economics

latter, if we want to have some goods and services, we produce them ourselves or buy them from someone else. In so doing, we weigh our own costs and benefits, we evaluate market prices, and, we make our own decisions. With governments however, be they small or large, local or national, our individual preferences and our individual decisions play a much reduced role–if they play a role at all. Governments are constituted to respond to a perceived majority, to the "voice of the people," to society.

As efficient as this may at first seem, the difficulty with this single voice, in the context of professor Friedman's example (see page 29), is that it can negate the great advantage of a market economy. Recall that, in a market economy, "Each man can vote, as it were, for the color of tie he wants and get it" while those in the political minority "submit." In other words, political decisions made in response to the desires of the perceived majority simply cannot please as many people as do individual decisions made in the market.

Also, it is simply not possible to construct what economists call a "collective preference scale"–or a consistent set of majority preferences–from sets of individual preferences. For example, consider the case of three individuals–Larry, Curly, and Moe–who express their preferences for three different government programs (A, B, and C), by listing them 1, 2, and 3, with number one being the most preferable:

	Programs		
	A	B	C
Larry	1	2	3
Curly	3	1	2
Moe	2	3	1

Clearly program A is preferred to program B, because both Larry and Moe like it better; only Curly doesn't. And program B is preferred to program C, because Larry and Curly like it better; only Moe doesn't. So, if A is better than B, and B is better than C, A wins as the most preferred program, right?

Wrong!

Another look at the above preferences tables shows us that program C is actually preferred to program A. Both Curly and Moe like it better, only Larry doesn't. And around and around we go. So much for democracy! Good and desirable as it is, it doesn't solve our problem here.

Compounding all this, it turns out that many public decision makers represent a relatively small minority of the population. For instance, let's suppose that a politician (or a particular party's nominee, as in the case of a Presidential election) was elected by a respectable 55 percent of the votes cast in a recent election. Yet, if voter turnout for that election was only 60 percent, it turns out that the elected official received the support of only one-third (.55 times .60) of the registered voters. If the number of registered voters in the region was about one-third of the population, the politician will be making decisions on behalf of 11 percent or so of the people in the district. And, if these decisions transcend local or state boundaries, so that they affect people who had no chance to participate in the election, then . . . (but you get the idea).

The bottom line, so to speak, is that decisions made on behalf of others and in the public interest and are simply not as efficient as those made by the individuals themselves. All of the logic and all of the evidence, with the exception of the category of public goods, tell us that it is difficult, if not impossible, for politicians to spend our tax dollars as efficiently as we could do for ourselves. This is further compounded by decision makers who may not even represent a majority of their constituents.

Externalities

Decisions made by governments often have unwanted side effects–a concern in all decision making–that can become especially troublesome. For example, a rise in the national minimum wage, instead of guaranteeing the poorest workers a better income, may throw some of them out of work entirely, if their employers can no longer afford to keep them on.

Or a local rent control law, intended to benefit low income families by prohibiting the raising of their rents, often encourages landlords to let their low rent housing units deteriorate beyond habitability, or even to abandon them entirely. As a result, the very people who were supposed to reap the benefits of rent control may end up homeless out on the streets. As California biologist Garrett Hardin has pointed out, "It's impossible to do just one thing."

When we add the difficulty of unwanted externalities to the relative inefficiency of government decisions, the case for government involvement or action outside of its traditional role of supplying public goods becomes increasingly tenuous. In the end, when parties affected by a decision do not participate in the making of that decision (whether voluntarily or not), any unwanted side effects seem to have a greater inclination to outweigh the intended beneficial effects. No wonder so many people seem to disagree with so many decisions made by our elected officials!

The Federal Budget

Even so, government (and life) goes on, and so we turn our attention to the largest of all governments, the federal government. In this context, the federal budget–the annual document proposed by the President and approved by Congress–provides a useful point of departure when talking about government finances.

Where The Federal Dollar Comes From . . .

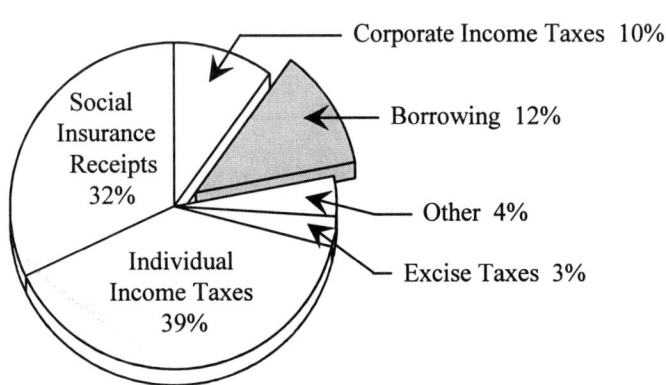

Annual federal budgets normally report revenues and expenditures in terms of mind-boggling numbers. However, the dollar amounts can be converted into percentages which change little from year to year, thereby allowing us to focus on the sources and uses of the typical federal dollar.[1]

As can be seen, individual income taxes and social insurance (Social Security) receipts together account for 71 percent of all federal revenues. The corporate income tax accounts for 10 percent of the total, with minor amounts from excise taxes (taxes on the manufacture or sale of certain items such as gasoline, tobacco, and liquor) and other sources such as customs duties, inheritance taxes, and so on. The third largest source of revenue, and the one most dangerous over time, is the 12 percent the government borrows from the private sector, primarily in the form of government bonds, notes, Treasury bills, and U.S. Government savings bonds. This annual borrowing is known as the federal deficit.

When we examine how the typical federal dollar is spent, we find that the categories range from a low of 1 percent on international affairs to a high of 22 percent on Social Security, with approximately equal amounts being spent on national defense, medicare and medicaid, and interest on the federal debt (where the debt is the sum of the annual deficits).

... And How The Federal Dollar is Spent

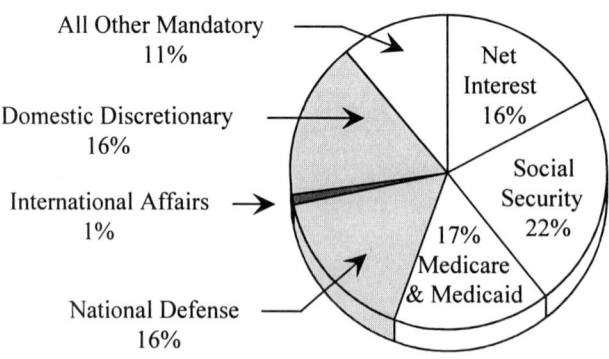

Another way to view federal expenditures is to separate the discretionary (shaded) from the mandatory (unshaded) expenditures. The mandatory spending–representing approximately two-thirds of

---

[1] Budget of the United States Government, Fiscal Year 1996.

all federal spending–is money that the federal government spends automatically unless the President and Congress take specific actions to stop it. This spending includes interest on the federal debt, Social Security payments, payments for medicare and medicaid, plus some other mandatory items. Discretionary spending–about one-third of the entire federal budget–is the amount that Congress and the President vote on each year.

Discretionary Fiscal Policy

Fiscal policies, the use of government spending and revenue collection measures to influence the economy, are created by members of the legislative and executive branches of our federal government, the people who work on Capitol Hill and in the White House. Their jobs depend on votes. In pursuing the will of the people and the special interests of their constituents, these decision makers naturally tend to favor government spending programs and to fear imposing taxes. As a result, our federal government is almost always running in the red and having to borrow money. The figure on page 53, which shows that approximately 12 percent of every federal dollar is borrowed, is only part of a long story. In fact, the historical record on this score is remarkable: President Lyndon Johnson was the last president (and a Democrat at that!) to have a federal budget surplus–and that was way back in 1969!

In addition, efforts to mobilize this discretionary part of the federal budget, to formulate a cogent and responsive economic policy, more often than not create political quagmires and gridlocks that far outlive the economic problems confronted in the first place. For example, by the time the bids have been received, the gauntlet of government rules and regulations successfully endured, the contracts let, and the construction workers finally start to be paid, years will have gone by and the original the economic problem (usually unemployment) that was supposed to be solved by a government construction project may have long since become history.

When we put it all together–all the federal taxing, borrowing, spending, subsidizing, penalizing, regulating, etc.–whether they are economically discretionary or not, these activities have an enormous impact on the economy. Closing military bases, threatening to discontinue or to reduce medicaid or agricultural price supports, and denying funding to state universities, among many such budgetary moves, all have traumatic impacts on the communities involved. Even if their collective impact leaves the impression that they seem to be less of a conscious and coordinated fiscal policy and more like an uncoordinated and unplanned fiscal circumstance, they are still important. After all, as we have already noted, the federal government is the single biggest player in our economy.

In practice, discretionary fiscal policy is less discretionary than most people might imagine. Despite many well-intended attempts to control federal spending, the political incentives are such that budgets are in deficit and, as a result, the total federal government debt grows apace, year after year. As of late, even the process of agreeing on a budget has become contentious, resulting in short-lived government shutdowns which were engineered in an attempt to force a particular point of view during the budgetary debate. Such actions are hardly efficient, let alone being in "the public interest"–and they will hardly solve our budgetary problems.

Our governments, like most governments in the world, have taken on a myriad of different large and small responsibilities, from national defense to aiding families with dependent children, from building roads and operating schools to selling petroleum drilling rights and regulating barber shops. All of these activities have economic impacts, and more than a few of us spend the larger part of our private and business lives dealing with them. While we can hardly analyze them all here, suffice it to say that, for better or for worse, when governments do something, it is presented as being done in the public interest, which means that it will be done differently than when individual motives and individual decision making are at work.

Admittedly, many clever people are able to use governments for their own personal ends, by bending government programs to their own needs, by legally or illegally manipulating government officials, or by paying for favors. Indeed, a great deal of business activity is focused on just such activities, and many businesses sink or swim on the basis of their relationship to a federal, state, or local government. But the mission of governments, officially and ideologically, if not always in practice, is to further the public, not the private good.

Of all of our various governments, our federal government–because of its national reach–is the one most concerned with trying to steer our economy in the direction of stable, healthy, and steady growth. In doing so, its behavior is analogous to the behavior of a host at a cocktail party, who is concerned that the guests are having a happy and convivial time. The trick is to know how to provide just the right amount of levity. The guests should not be just standing around with their hands in their pockets; neither should they become so rowdy that the neighbors have to call the cops. At cocktail parties, this trick is often accomplished by knowing exactly how stiff to mix the drinks. In our national economy, it is not quite so simple.

Mandatory Spending?

Two-thirds of federal government spending–the unshaded portion of the figure on page 54–is commonly called mandatory spending because it includes programs that are seemingly carved in stone, as politically untouchable *entitlements*. These entitlements–primarily Social Security, medicare, and medicaid–are programs which ensure payments when people qualify for already-established standards such as age or income. Medicare, for example, is a federal program available to all senior citizens regardless of income. Social Security is another program for which people qualify as soon as they reach a certain age. As a result of these criteria, spending in many categories is in response to events and forces that are generally beyond economic considerations. Even some traditionally discretionary categories, such as military outlays, are nearly untouchable, leaving much less for Congress and the President to determine every year.

Many of these mandatory expenditures also fall under the heading of *transfer payments,* payments for which the government receives neither goods nor services in return. Social Security payments, Aid to Families with Dependent Children (AFDC), and some forms of unemployment insurance payments are examples of transfer payments. Basically, these programs are designed to protect families and/or individuals from adverse economic circumstances which are presumed to be beyond their control.

Mandatory expenditures attract a lot of bad press in many circles, and they are often blamed for the reason why the federal budget is so difficult to balance. There is some truth in this, of course, but we also need to remember that any federal program or expenditure, with the possible exception of interest on the national debt, can be altered if Congress and the President have the will to do so. As a result, politicians who claim that it is not possible to rein in programs whose expenditures are getting out of hand, on the grounds that the spending is mandatory, are really abrogating their responsibilities and pandering to special interest groups.

The most pressing problem of this kind is the result of our aging population. For example, at the beginning of this century only one in twenty-five Americans was over the age of sixty-five. By the year 2040, one out of every four or five will have reached this golden age, causing a painful increase in our national dependency ratio–the ratio of the number of children and elderly for every 100 persons in the working-age brackets of 18 through 64 (this ratio was approximately 63 in 1997 and is expected to reach 78 by the year 2040). And, if we think kids are expensive to take care of, try a growing population of retirees, getting older and sicker with every birthday, but voting for their own interests on election day more assiduously than any other voting block.

The "mother" of all such mandatory expenditure problems, however, is the annual interest our federal government has to pay on its accumulated debt. The political failures that have created this problem have been described above. They remain the quintessential malfunction of a democracy where getting elected or reelected may seem more important to some politicians than making responsible decisions–in this case, creating a responsibly balanced government budget.

Of course, not all mandatory spending is bad. Many of the expenditures, and some of the revenue collection mechanisms, fall into the category of *automatic stabilizers*, programs that automatically trigger benefits if changes in the economy adversely threaten people's economic well-being. For example, a worker unable to find employment after getting laid off can soon file for unemployment benefits (although workers who are fired because of misconduct or who quit without good reason are generally ineligible for these benefits). Theoretically, these benefits are large enough to enable the worker to get by until new employment is found, yet still small enough to encourage the worker to seek new employment.

The progressive income tax is another mechanism that enhances economic stability. A worker in the 28 percent marginal tax bracket may suddenly find him or herself in a higher tax bracket if income goes up, or in a lower bracket if income suddenly goes down. The progressive nature of the personal income tax thus tends to moderate sudden and unexpected changes in income, dampening at the top while protecting at the bottom.

The advantages of these automatic stabilizers, then, is that they are far more responsive to changes in the economy than are programs that rely on congressional approval, bids, suitable weather before construction can begin, and so on. The responses are immediate, targeted to those groups where they will do the intended good, and fully automatic.

Thinking Like an Economist

Perhaps nothing makes it clearer that ours is a free enterprise, market economy than when we try to apply government controls to it. In spite of the fact that government–all federal, state, and local governments taken together–is such a big player, our economy is still primarily the product of the myriad of decisions taken individually by hundreds of millions of Americans every day. In this regard, the body economic is less like our own bodies, in which our heads pretty much rule what happens in the rest of our bodies, and more like a coral reef, which just changes and grows, according to the behavior of the hundreds of millions of individual coral polyps that form the body of the reef.

Politics can seem much more complicated than economics. The motives for behavior certainly go far beyond anything as simple as maximizing the usefulness of a consumer budget or maximizing the profitability of a business enterprise. Power, prestige, public image, carefully positioning oneself on important issues, and outmaneuvering opponents are much more obvious ingredients in all political relationships. Non-economic, even heroic performances may occasionally be called for.

And yet, politicians are not normally fools. Furthermore, their vast armies of nonpolitical, ordinary employees in all of our local, state, and federal governments are just that: ordinary working people. They and the politicians are just as likely as anybody else to make the very best possible use of the economic way of thinking. What this usually comes down to for all of them is keeping and advancing in the government job, winning the next election, and hanging on to that house or apartment in town, in the state capital, or in Washington, D.C. The best way to do this, as always, is to keep abreast of developments, take advantage of opportunities, and keep decisions incremental, so that careful adjustments can be made along the way.

All of which is, in fact, thinking like an economist. However, instead of its being focused on maximizing consumer satisfactions or producer profits, this thinking is focused on getting reelected, achieving better performance reviews, and being appointed to better positions. Serving the public well is usually–but not always!–the best way of accomplishing these ends.

The nature of government decisions may not yield the same level of satisfaction that we receive when we make them ourselves (is less government better than more?), but they must be made and so we tolerate them. Besides, those public goods, the ones that would not ordinarily be sufficiently provided by the private economy, are still needed.

Chapter 8

MONEY AND MONETARY POLICY

> *Money, it turned out, was exactly like sex, you thought of nothing else if you didn't have it and thought of other things if you did.*
> – *James Arthur Baldwin (1924-), American novelist*

Economists like to divide our national economic policy into two categories: fiscal policy, named after the taxing and spending activities of the federal government during its budgetary fiscal year; and monetary policy, meaning the various banking and financial activities of the Federal Reserve System. Of course, the two categories often overlap, as, for example, when the federal government has to borrow money, in order to finance its spending, and the banks of the Federal Reserve System adjust their policies, in order to accommodate this borrowing. Anyway, fiscal and monetary policies should always work together towards the same national economic objectives. At least, the right hand should know what the left hand is doing.

Increasingly, the failure or inability of government to manage the economy through its fiscal policy leaves the Federal Reserve System and its monetary policy tools holding the bag. Given the importance of this System, it is surprising that so few Americans know much or care much about it. Our story, however, begins with money and its importance in the economy.

Dollars and Cents

Contrary to the cliché, money doesn't make the world go around. In a sense, money is just talk, and in the economic world–

just as in all the rest of our world–talk is not as important as action. But, as all of us who have to deal with other people know, talk can be mighty useful. And so is money.

First of all, like talk, money is a means of communication. It communicates the market values (prices) of even the most completely unrelated things to even the most completely unrelated people in the marvelously common language of dollars and cents. As such, we could say that money serves as a measure of value.

Secondly, it can serve as a temporary reservoir, or store, of value. That is, the use of it can be postponed for transactions that take place in the future. If invested, a store of money may accumulate into larger funds, which may be especially useful, either because a larger fund will be needed to get the job done, or because the money can be put to better use at a later date, or both.

And finally, money is useful, because it can be transferred from one owner to another, as a gift, or in response to being taxed or being expropriated in some other way, or as part of the give and take of an exchange. In this regard, money serves its most useful function of all–as a medium of exchange.

In spite of all this usefulness of money, however, it is best to remember that it doesn't have any real substance of its own. Even large gold and silver coins that may have a soul-satisfying heft to them usually have metallic values that differ wildly from the monetary values imprinted on their sides. In this regard, again, money is like talk. This becomes a very useful analogy, as we describe the Federal Reserve System and how money is created.

The Federal Reserve System

The Federal Reserve System consists of twelve Federal Reserve Banks, each in its own district, with all twelve districts covering the entire United States. Historically, each of these twelve Federal Reserve Banks enjoyed some autonomy in dealing with the local economic conditions of their districts, but today all ultimately act in concert with one another. If anything, the Federal Reserve Bank of New York, being in the financial center of the economy, is probably the most influential.

Remarkably, the Federal Reserve System is not even owned by the government, but is instead organized as a stock corporation that is owned by its member banks. Given the importance of the institution, however, Congress has determined that the management of the Fed be conducted by a seven-member Board of Governors, each of whom is nominated by the President and confirmed by Congress. The Board is located in Washington, D.C. where it conducts its monetary policy and oversees all twelve banks. The Chairman of Board of Governors, as relatively unknown to the general public as he or she may be, is arguably the second most powerful person in America.

Probably the closest contact any of us have with the Federal Reserve Banks comes through their currency, the Federal Reserve Notes, that we carry around in our wallets and purses. Approximately $350 billion of such greenbacks are held around the world, over half of them outside the United States, which, by the way, we can take as a nice authentication of the global respect our dollar enjoys. However, as we might guess from our own family finances, most of the American money in existence–about ninety percent of it–isn't in the form of such cash. Instead, it is on deposit in our various checking, savings, time, and money market fund accounts, which is to say that it exists as electronic blips in computers and occasionally sees the light of day as printed numbers on our bank statements and as dollars and cents written or printed on the many trillions of checks that we Americans send and receive each year. All these forms of money, including coins (issued by the U.S. Treasury), comprise the total quantity of money in the economy.

Here's how it works. Our various neighborhood banks, big city banks, investment houses, credit unions, and so on provide us with the services we need to establish and to use our various kinds of accounts. They don't do this out of the goodness of their hearts. They need to be paid, and the way this is accomplished is to lend out at interest most–ninety percent and more–of the money we have on deposit with them. It's our money that they are lending, but we don't even notice it, because rarely do all of us depositors, *en masse*, want to withdraw more money than we have on deposit at any one time. For the most part, a ten percent or less reserve at the bank would be more than sufficient to cover our withdrawals. In the rare case when it would not be sufficient, one bank (or more likely the Fed) can always help another cover these withdrawals with a temporary loan.

When banks lend out our money, the money ends up doing double, triple, and multiple duty. The borrower, of course, knows that the money isn't his or hers, and that it must ultimately be repaid. But the borrower borrowed the money in order to spend it, perhaps on a new car, a new home, some urgent medical treatments; or for new factory plant and equipment. And the seller of these goods and services receives this money as income and, most likely, will deposit it into his or her (or its) bank account. So now two depositors believe that they own the money (and they do)! The seller's bank, of course, treats this new deposit as any other deposit, and lends almost all of it out to yet another willing borrower, and around we go again.

If the economy is booming, consumers and businesses are eager spenders and borrowers. If a single dollar is deposited in a bank subject to a 10 percent reserve requirement, 10 percent, or $.10 must be set aside and $.90 can be loaned out. When that loan reenters the banking system as a new deposit, 90 percent of it can be lent out, and so on until eventually $10 of deposits ($1.00 + .90 + .81 + .729 + ... + .00 = $10.00) are created as shown in the figure below:

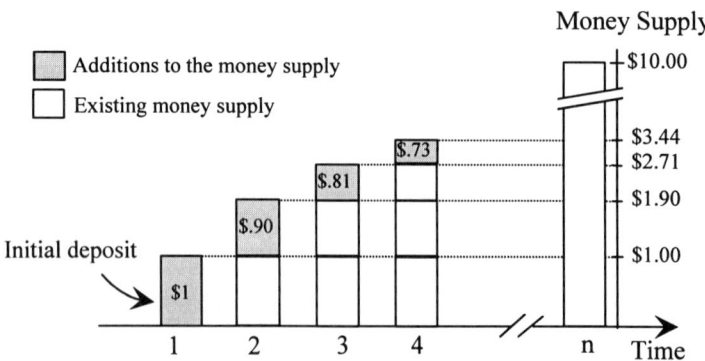

By the same arithmetic, if the economy is in recession and business is bad, consumers and businesses may have to withdraw some money from their bank deposits, and a single dollar withdrawal, by reducing the bank's ability to lend money, can collapse the potential bank deposits by $10 (or, -$1.00 - .90 - .81 - .729 - ... - .00 = -$10.00).

So, the quantity of money in existence at any one time has little to do with the amount of Federal Reserve currency in circulation, and mostly to do with how actively consumers and businesses are borrowing and banks are lending. Indeed, by writing checks, depositing money into banks, and borrowing from banks, the quantity of money seems to be largely our own creation. It can grow and shrink, appearing and disappearing out of nowhere, like the animated talk at a cocktail party. So, while we can't write checks against money we don't have on deposit, banks can earn revenue by lending a large proportion of our deposits to borrowers–allowing the money supply to expand and contract, adjusting to the level of this activity.

Monetary Policy

So where does the Federal Reserve System come in? Is the quantity of money in America out of its hands? Like an incompetent host at the previously mentioned cocktail party, is the "Fed" unable either to stimulate the guests to animated conversation or to prevent them from becoming too rowdy?

Neither. The Fed has three major party control tactics up its sleeves, and these tactics form the basis of its monetary policy. First and most commonly used is the Fed's enormous power to influence the size of our individual bank accounts, by buying from us or selling to us U.S. Government securities such as Treasury bills and bonds. In fact, the money supply increases whenever the Fed buys assets from the private sector, and the money supply contracts whenever it sells assets to the private sector.

Here is how it works. If the Federal Reserve perceives that the economy is drifting towards recession–if the cocktail guests are standing around with their hands in their pockets–it will buy some government securities from people and businesses who happen to own them. They will be willing to sell, because the Fed buys the securities at auction on the open New York bond market and it can always offer a price that the sellers can't reasonably refuse. The reason that the Fed can do this is because the very securities it buys are the assets against which new Federal Reserve Notes or, more likely, Federal Reserve Bank checks are issued as payment. In this sense the Federal Reserve System can create as much new money as it wants. No other agency of the government, no business, and certainly no one of us can do the same. The new money received in this way by the sellers will most likely be deposited in the sellers' banks, where it will burn a hole in bankers' pockets until it has been profitably lent out, which should help to get the party going again.

Essentially, then, monetary policy is a supply and demand situation–with the Fed in charge of the supply. The interest rate that banks charge when loans are made is simply the price of credit. If the Fed can successfully increase the money supply as shown in the illustration below, then the impact is to lower interest rates all across the economy:

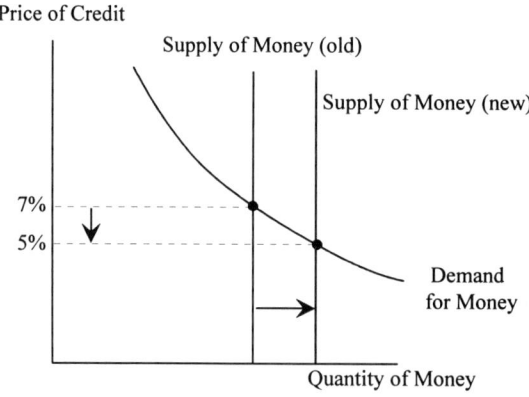

Should the Fed perceive the opposite problem, that the economy is becoming overheated and inflationary–that the party is becoming too rowdy–it can shift this open market policy into reverse by selling off some government securities from its vast inventory. The people and businesses that buy these securities almost certainly will pay for them with checks drawn against their bank deposits. As a result, the banks will have less money to lend. With this diminution of money in circulation and on deposit in banks, businesses and consumers begin to feel the pinch of "tight money," which is another way of saying that interest rates are high. So, they borrow less and spend less, and the party becomes less rowdy.

In case all this open market policy doesn't do the trick, or in case it is an inappropriate tactic for other reasons, the Fed can turn to its second monetary ploy, the discount rate. This is the interest rate the Fed charges our neighborhood and city banks when they borrow in order to meet seasonal lending needs or to cover an unexpected shortage of reserves. As mentioned before, they can borrow from other banks, but their district's Federal Reserve Bank is their lender of last resort. If the Fed charges a high rate of interest–a high discount rate–for such a loan, banks are discouraged from borrowing. Conversely, if the Fed offers loans at low discount rates, banks may borrow enthusiastically to expand their loans and investments. Most importantly, since the Fed is the biggest and most powerful of all our nation's banks, the other banks usually follow the Fed's lead. So, even though the Fed may not change its discount rate very often– perhaps only once or twice a year–its discount rate policy will exert a strong influence on the interest rate policies of all banks.

The third tactic of the Fed, used rarely, but potentially very powerful, is to change the legal requirement for the proportion of deposits that banks have to keep on reserve. Like the posted speed limits on our roads and highways, the legal reserve requirement during the early years of the Fed was unrealistically restrictive, requiring banks to hold in reserve a larger proportion of their customers' deposits than would be necessary for safe bank operations. But, unlike the speed limits, the legal reserve requirement has to be obeyed.

In more recent years, in response to growing competition in America's banking industry and in accord with the prevailing political spirit of deregulation, the legal reserve requirement has been gradually lowered and made less restrictive. This has certainly contributed to a stimulation of increased levity in the American economic cocktail party, over what it would have been without this liberalization. In the unlikely event that the reserve requirement would be raised and made more restrictive, banks would have to build up their reserves and reduce their outstanding loans and investments, imposing a powerfully restrictive restraint on the economy.

And these are the means by which our monetary policy is carried out. Do they work? We might as well ask if the glass is half full or half empty. Recessions and inflations, while somewhat milder in recent years, still continue to torment our mostly free enterprise

American economy, and our economic growth rate of around one to three percent per year has not been among the world's more rapid rates. But our American economy is still the world's biggest, one of the world's most eager for new kinds of enterprise, and, as a result, one of the most advanced economies. It is also among the world's most stable economies. Along with our steady democracy and good, if not yet perfect, record for civil liberties and justice, America is a global magnet for investment and for immigration. Our monetary policy is a big part of this picture. It must be doing something right.

Thinking Like an Economist

Of course, monetary policy has an impact. When the Fed buys securities, lowers the discount rate, and reduces the reserve requirement, the increased availability of money and lower interest rates tempt consumers and businesses to borrow and spend. Conversely, when the Fed sells securities, raises the discount rate, and increases the reserve requirement, the decreased availability of money and higher interest rates will cause consumers and businesses to think twice, before borrowing and spending. This has a big impact, because, as we emphasized before, people and businesses proceed incrementally–thinking like an economist as we might say–as they weigh the changing costs of borrowing against the available benefits to be received or given up.

Monetary policy, both for those few officials who make it and for those many of the rest of us who try to understand it, is best thought of an economic and political art, rather than as a purely scientific or mechanical function. Regardless of which way we think of it, however, we do have to take it into account very seriously. Tightening up the monetary policy screws, or loosening them just a little, can make a big difference in the outlook for business profits, the investment climate, and the willingness of consumers to go into debt to buy a house or other big ticket item. In this sense, it is best to think of our national monetary policy not only as responding to the prevailing economic climate, but also as creating some economic weather of its own. It pays to watch it carefully.

Chapter 9

MEASURING ECONOMIC PERFORMANCE

There are two kinds of statistics, the kind you look up and the kind you make up.

— *Rex Stout (1886-1975), American novelist*

When it comes to economic statistics, these days we are seeing less of the made-up kind, in large part because so many of the communist governments and dictatorships around the world have gone out of business. The intentional falsification of productivity data, unemployment and inflation rates, and so on–all for propaganda purposes–are simply less prevalent than several decades ago. Among its many other virtues, freedom also seems to be a powerful invitation to honesty.

In the industrialized nations of the free world, emphatically including our United States, the intended purpose of our economic statistics has always been to provide us with an honest and accurate representation of the true state of our economic affairs. Not that they always succeed one hundred percent! Truth is often changing and elusive. But if the consumer price index turns out to have overstated inflation in recent years (and there is considerable evidence that it has), or if our international trade statistics have failed to take some important exports into account, it is not for lack of trying to achieve accuracy.

In fact, our economic statistics are highly credible, easily available, very useful, and surprisingly interesting–once we get to know them.

How We Got Here From There

Economists, it seems, have always had a thing for numbers. In the early 1800s, some economists recognized (or thought they recognized) recurrent periods of economic expansion and contraction that we now call the business cycle. However, the early writers had to do more than claim that the economy had a tendency to go up and down with some degree of regularity. They had to find or develop sources of continuous, reliable data that would show the overall movement of the economy.

Out of necessity (if not convenience), economists often used whatever statistical series were at hand. Some examined historical records such as pig iron consumption, wages and unemployment rates, and even per capita beer consumption. Stanley Jevons, the British economist and statistician, even associated changes in overall economic performance with sunspot activities in the late 1800s–a proposition for which he was roundly ridiculed, even though later economists conceded some validity to his arguments.

The search for reliable statistical data that could be used for predictive, explanatory, and diagnostic purposes was in full swing by the turn of the century. By then, economists in a number of countries had developed some fairly sophisticated series such as indices concerning real (adjusted for inflation) aggregate money wages, price levels, and a host of other measures that covered all manner of manufactured and agricultural commodities.

The Search for Leading Indicators

The study of business cycles, and the search for statistical series that could be used to predict them, became particularly intense in the United States. By 1920, Wesley Mitchell had founded the National Bureau of Economic Research (NBER), which went on to examine the relationship of thousands of individual data series to the overall performance of the economy. Those which tended to go up and down with the economy with some degree of regularity were then identified as "leading," "lagging," or "coincident" indicators.

To illustrate, suppose that the shaded areas in the illustration on the next page represents brief periods of economic decline, while the unshaded areas represent periods of growth. If the horizontal axis represents time, then it should be clear that the economy is moving from periods of expansion to recession and then into expansion again as we move from left to right. Also note that we know nothing about the magnitudes of these periods–the relative strength or weakness of the economy–except for the length of time the economy is in one phase or the other.

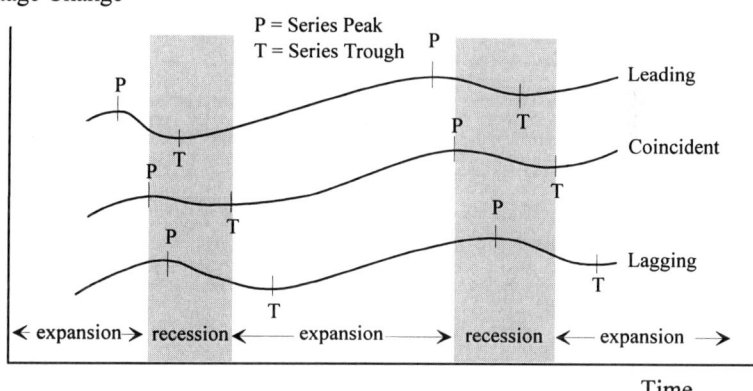

Next, and in the tradition of the NBER, we superimpose a series such as the unemployment rate, the prime rate charged by banks, or some other series that might tend to move in some pattern that is consistent with the direction of the overall economy. For example, if a series tends to generally turn down (get worse) before the economy enters a recession, and if the series tends to generally turn up (get better) before the economy enters a period of recovery, the series would be classified as a *leading* economic indicator. Another series, however, might turn down as the economy turns down, and then up as the economy turns up–which would classify it as a *coincident* indicator. Even other series may turn only after the economy turns, thereby making it a *lagging* economic indicator.

Eventually, and only after thousands of series were examined, only a handful were found to behave more or less consistently as leading indicators. The handful actually numbers about 60, but some of these series overlap as in the case of corporate profits which are measured once in current (inflation distorted) dollars, and then again in terms of constant (inflation adjusted) dollars. Other measures are rather arcane, such as the ratio of price to unit labor costs for nonfarm businesses, and are seldom reported in the press although they are followed by many experts.

The more visible, and oft-cited, series are listed in the table on the next page. The table also shows the three-part classification given to each series. These designations–"L" for leading, "Lg" for lagging, "C" for coincident, and "U" for unclassified–describe how an individual series generally (although not always) performs over the course of the business cycle.

Some series, such as the average weekly hours in manufacturing employment, is a leading indicator for both recessions and expansions (and therefore a leading indicator in an overall sense), earning a designation of L,L,L. Other series, like the help-wanted ads in newspapers, leads the economy when it comes to predicting recessions, but lags when it comes to predicting expansions, giving it a classification of L,Lg,U (the last "U" designates that it is an unclassified indicator overall). Even other series, such as capacity utilization rates, generally turn down before the economy turns down, and then recover only when the economy recovers–thereby earning a L,C,U classification.

Finding Safety in Numbers

Finally, why do we use so many series to predict changes in the direction of aggregate economic activity? In other words, why not just use one or two and simplify the analysis? The answer is that no single series is reliable all of the time. To work around this problem, several series are selected from each of the major economic process areas, and are then combined into a composite index currently known as the *index of 10 leading indicators.*

On balance, the combination of 10 several such series is more reliable than is any single series at a given time, although timing is still a bit of a problem. For example, on average, the leading index turns down about 13 months before the economy actually begins to enter a recession–although the warning may be as short as eight months or as long as 20 months (and even these numbers are subject

Chapter 9: Measuring Economic Performance   73

Selected Leading Indicators

	— Series Timing —
Major Economic Process Areas:	Recessions, Expansions, Overall
Employment and Unemployment	
*Average weekly hours of employment in manufacturing	L,L,L
Average weekly overtime employment hours, manufacturing	L,C,L
*Average weekly initial unemployment claims	L,C,L
Help-wanted ads in newspapers	L,Lg,U
Unemployment rate	L,Lg,U
Production	
Capacity utilization rate, manufacturing	L,C,U
Capacity utilization rate, materials	L,C,U
Consumption, Trade, Orders, and Deliveries	
Manufacturers' new orders, durable goods	L,L,L
*Mfrs.' new orders, constant dollars, consumer goods & materials	L,L,L
Change in manufacturers' unfilled orders, durable goods	L,L,L
*Vendor performance–slower deliveries	L,L,L
Personal consumption expenditures, automobiles	L,C,C
*Index of consumer expectations	L,L,L
Fixed Capital Investment	
Net business formations	L,L,L
New business incorporations	L,L,L
*Contracts and orders for plant and equipment	L,L,L
*Building permits for new private housing units	L,L,L
Inventories and Inventory Adjustment	
Change in business inventories in constant dollars	L,L,L
Prices, Costs, and Profits	
Change in sensitive materials prices	L,L,L
*Stock prices, 500 common stocks	L,L,L
Corporate profits after tax	L,L,L
Money and Credit	
Change in money supply M1	L,L,L
*Money supply M2 in constant dollars	L,L,L
Net change in mortgage debt	L,L,L
Net change in consumer installment credit	L,L,L
Change in business and consumer credit outstanding	L,L,L
Delinquency rate, installment loans	L,L,L

(*) Series also included in the composite *index of 10 leading indicators*

to change as the government revises its historical data). The ability of the leading index to forecast the end of a recession (the beginning of a recovery) is even more limited, because the average warning is only 3 months with a range of from 1 to 10 months.

Economists are prone to argue about the overall usefulness of the leading index, with most of the debate focusing on the variability of the warning time it provides. Consequently, exclusive use of the leading index to forecast the exact timing of an impending change in the direction of overall economic activity is chancy at best, making it a real adventure for forecasters whose living depends on making accurate economic predictions.

So good economic forecasters seldom rely on this tool alone. Well over a hundred other well-established coincident and even lagging economic indicators are examined as well. Also, highly mathematical econometric models that digest all this information in computer programs are often used to lend a sense of scientific accuracy to the forecasting processes. But, in the end, the gut feelings and the intuition that develop with years of forecasting experience continue to be very influential. Economic forecasting, like all forecasting, remains as much an art as a science.

What About the Level of Economic Activity?

All of the series identified as leading, lagging, or coincident indicators have a decided drawback–they can be used to help predict the *direction* (up or down) of economic activity, but they are of little help when it comes to predicting the *level* of economic activity. In other words, we might conclude that the economy is doing better, if the average number of weekly employment hours in manufacturing is increasing. Or, we might conclude the economy is doing worse, if the length of the average workweek is falling. But how much better or worse was unknown, because economists lacked a way to measure the overall level, or magnitude, of economic activity.

All that changed when John Maynard Keynes published his magnificent *General Theory of Employment, Interest, and Money* in 1936. In what has been regarded as perhaps one of the most influential books written in the 20th century, Keynes went on to describe the overall economy as the sum of its parts, which he identified as the consumer (C), investment (I), government (G), and foreign (F) sectors. The sum of these parts was called Gross National Product, or GNP for short, so that the relationship of the individual sectors to the sum of the whole is written as GNP = C + I + G + F.

GDP and All That

The concept of GNP, recently changed to GDP for Gross *Domestic* Product, is the dollar sum of all goods and services produced within a country's borders in a year, regardless of who owns the resources (so all of the cars produced in a Japanese-owned Toyota plant in Kentucky are included in GDP whereas the output of a U.S.-owned firm in Toronto is not). There are some serious inadequacies in GDP accounting such as the exclusion of unpaid homemaker services–things like washing, cooking, doing homework with the kids and so on–but, all in all, it is a wonderful measure of the overall level of economic activity and one that will be with us for the foreseeable future.

In fact, when Keynes first proposed the concept, economists all over the world and especially those in the United States scrambled to develop statistical measures that would prove or disprove his views. Ultimately, the stimulus provided by Keynes led to the development of the national income and product accounts that are now maintained by the U.S. Department of Commerce. The monthly and quarterly reports of these accounts–GDP, personal income, national income, personal consumption expenditures, and corporate profits, to name just a few of the major ones–are eagerly awaited by business decision makers, politicians, economists, and people of all persuasions.

GDP is, in many ways, the integrative link of our economic statistics, because it provides the missing measure of the level of economic activity. GDP is what we seek to both measure and forecast with our economic statistics, and it has become the main measure of the economy's health. If GDP is going up, we are better off; it is going down, we're in trouble. All of the many economic fixes proposed by our politicians–flat taxes, rescinding the capital gains tax, new tariffs and import quotas, etc.–in order to "grow the economy" will ultimately show up in the GDP statistics. It's a series that bears watching.

Thinking Like an Economist

The economic way of thinking is based on incremental decision making that weighs the marginal benefits of an action against its marginal costs. Such decisions require good information, information often found in the form of our economic statistics. Economic statistics are the foundation for economic forecasts and predictions. But they also tell us where we are and how we are doing, which is to say that they are the measures of our economic performance. Without them we could hardly be expected to know where we are going.

Economic statistics are the result of one of the more extraordinary human endeavors of our modern age. They are the *proprioceptors* of our body economic. That is, what our eyes and ears, the nerves in our limbs and torsos, and our brains signal to us about our bodies, economic statistics signal to us about our economy. They tell us what positions our body parts are in, so to speak, how our digestions are doing, whether we are tense or relaxed, hot or cold, and whether we are sick or healthy.

Obviously, the makers of our fiscal and monetary economic policies need to know these things about our economy, if they are to make effective economic policy. Equally obviously, all businesses and consumer decision makers should be aware of the state of the economy, especially when they make important decisions such as investing in a new business, buying a new home, or making a career change.

So, for all these reasons, it pays to keep our eyes on these measures of economic performance. It's easy to do: just keep an eye on the television and radio news, the papers and news magazines, or log on to one of the many world-wide web sites to keep abreast of our economic health.

Chapter 10

WORKING FOR A LIVING

From a brief exchange that took place between Calvin and his Dad while raking leaves in the yard:

Calvin: *I've decided I want to be millionaire when I grow up.*
Dad: *Well, you'll have to work pretty hard to get a million dollars.*
Calvin: *No I won't. You will.*
Dad: *Me?*
Calvin: *I just want to inherit it.*

–From "The Best of Calvin and Hobbes"

Among the many ways we have of making money, working for it wouldn't seem like anyone's first choice. Probably the best way is to have been born into it, to have always had enough family property and income generating investments, so that what we do with our lives never has to be ruled by the wages we are able to earn.

Wealth vs. Work

The freedom to live our lives independent of the constraints put on us by our wages is what's called being independently wealthy. Some people feel they have achieved this goal with a nest egg of only a few hundred thousand dollars; others have many millions and are still driven to accumulate further. Either way, however, building up a significant fund of income producing wealth–if we don't already have one–is the second most fundamental motive for working for pay. The first motive, of course, is to earn enough to make living possible and, beyond that, to make it enjoyable. For most people in America and everywhere else in the world, earning this income means working for it, whether we like it or not.

Work is distinguished from wealth, as a source of income, by our having to appear in person to perform the work. Our property and our investments can generate money and other benefits for us while we sleep or while we are touring the tropics, but, if we want to generate income by working, we have to show up ourselves to do the job. Since this usually takes up a large part of most of the days of every week, our lives become largely defined by what kind of work we do and how much income it produces.

Our Pay Scale

It will come as no surprise that, generally, the more productive we are at work, the higher our wages will be. A hard working and highly creative aerospace engineer, let's say, can expect a bigger paycheck than a not-especially-enthusiastic security guard at a Wal-Mart in a low crime area. Furthermore, what we bring along with us to our jobs–our skills, education, experience, ability to interact effectively with other people, our attitudes, our creativity and intelligence, and, sometimes even our special tools, such as a mechanic's complete set of socket wrenches or a violinist's Stradivarius violin–will also increase the income we are likely to earn. In this sense, most of our wages are earned by the productive human and tangible capital we bring with us to our jobs, rather than by our human toil. In fact, such toil, all by itself, completely unskilled, inexperienced, unadorned, unmotivated and unaided, has a very low productivity and would receive very little compensation–certainly less that the legal minimum wage–if it could find an employment opportunity at all.

But being productive is only the first prerequisite for earning a high wage. It is also necessary that there not be too many similarly productive workers competing for the same opportunities. Even the aforementioned aerospace engineers can become a dime a dozen, so to speak, if there is a very large number of them all holding or seeking employment in the same labor market at the same time. Employers tend to pay all their factors of production–and that includes their employees–at a rate determined by the revenue productivity of the last unit hired. Economists cite the rule that factors of production get paid according to their marginal revenue productivities. What this means for our aerospace engineers is that, although the first and second ones working for a firm may be almost invaluable, the thirtieth engineer or the three hundredth does not produce nearly as much additional revenue for the firm. And, to the degree that all these engineers are interchangeable with one another, none of them can claim to be the first or the second. All of them have to accept a wage that is determined by the revenue productivity of the last aerospace engineer working for the firm. And, if there are a lot of them, none of them will get paid very much.

Scarcity, uniqueness, and exclusiveness, then, are also required for a high wage. Education is, perhaps, the most important way of achieving these. The more educated and the more uniquely valuable we become, the less likely we will be treated as interchangeable with a platoon of other workers, all driving down the marginal revenue productivity of the work we do. This explains why high school graduates earn much more than dropouts, and why college graduates earn much more than high school graduates.

Another way of achieving such uniqueness is through the application of some unique talent or characteristic, something for which a person is undeniably better than almost anyone else. This explains the astronomical salaries of some professional athletes, movie stars, fashion models, and entertainers. Those of us who may question the real productivity of a foul-mouthed recording idol or pornographic video star should be reminded that *revenue* productivity is the only kind of productivity that determines wage. The most uniquely talented and productive poet or scientist can't make a dime, if no one buys his or her poetry or science.

Another way to achieve higher wages is by purposely restricting the number of workers in our labor market. Lawyers restrict the practice of law to lawyers who have passed the bar examination. The medical profession limits entry even more effectively than the lawyers, because they deny the opportunity for education even *before* prospective entrants have a chance to take the certification exams. The law graduate, who has several years invested in a legal education, will study for and then take the bar exam as many times as possible, in order to complete the certification. The young (and often talented) applicants to medical school soon find another occupation, if they are denied admission to medical school. After all, they don't have as much time and effort invested as their pre-bar law counterparts. The difference between the lawyers and the doctors, then, is that the former puts the barriers to entry near the end of a person's preparation for the profession–while the doctors put the barrier to admission right up front.

Barriers abound, and restrictive licensing requirements are even used to limit the numbers of engineers, barbers, child care providers, life guards, truck drivers, elementary school teachers, and many other kinds of workers. And, of course, labor unions try to restrict all employment in their respective trades and industries to their own members.

Labor Unions

Labor unions do more than just try to limit the number of workers in their profession. Throughout their several centuries of history, their main function has been to compel employers to recognize the fact that there are real human beings attached to the labor force they have working for them in their factories and on their farms. People are more than just another factor of production. Working conditions–including occupational safety and the number of hours in a workday, the security of employment and seniority benefits, disability insurance and pensions, the number and duration of rest breaks and lunch breaks, and all those other considerations that can make working for a living more decent and humane–become labor union concerns.

Wages remain the main concern. Although economists theorize that all factors of production are paid according to their marginal revenue product, which is determined rather automatically by market forces, there is often quite a bit of room for negotiation. This is especially true for those workers who bring special craft skills to the job–carpenters, bakers, electricians, musicians, and so on–because they can negotiate from the strength of their own uniqueness. And the first successful American unions in the nineteenth century organized such workers into dozens of different craft unions. In 1886, under the inspired leadership of Samuel Gompers (a member of the cigar makers union), they joined together in an umbrella organization called the American Federation of Labor. Unionized labor was entering the mainstream of the American economy.

Later, as mass production industries began to dominate in the twentieth century, labor unions began to organize along industrial, rather than craft lines. The names of these unions, such as the United Auto Workers, United Steel Workers, and, more recently, the Farm Workers of America, signaled this inclusiveness. Under the impassioned leadership of John L. Lewis (a member of the United Mine Workers of America union), these industrial unions formed the Congress of Industrial Organizations. The Great Depression of the 1930s was raging, and, in an effort to support working people, New Deal government policies favored unions. The heyday of American labor unionism was beginning. By 1955, when the two labor union confederations merged as the AFL-CIO, the proportion of employed Americans who belonged to unions peaked at almost one-third. The trend, then, had been for labor union organizations to adjust successfully to the changing patterns of industrial structure.

In the second half of the twentieth century, however, success became more elusive. The labor unions did not join in the civil rights movement as enthusiastically as might have been expected for such workers' organizations. The accelerating changes in the structures of the American economy–especially the decline of the so-called smokestack industries, the rapid increases in the number of office workers, and the development of high technology industries–seemed to outpace their abilities to adjust.

Today, approximately fifteen percent of American workers belong to labor unions, a reduction in both relative and absolute numbers. However, their main function, to compel employers to recognize that there are real human beings attached to the labor force they have working for them, remains.

Thinking Like an Economist

Working is more fun than it used to be. There is much less heavy lifting, more central heating and air conditioning, better on-the-job safety, and, especially for those jobs that require post-secondary education, there are even some interesting things to do. Most Americans even identify themselves primarily by what job they hold, rather than by their religion, family role, or neighborhood. The old idea, central to Marxist theory, that all work is a burden and that we survive by the sweat of our brows, is gradually evaporating.

We might expect, then, that the more we are paid for our work, the more hours of labor we would be willing to supply. And, to some degree, this is the way it is: people with six-figure annual incomes–think of medical doctors, upper echelon executives, top performing agents and sales representatives–often work 16 hours a day, six days per week, while the rest of us figure a 40-hour week is plenty.

But that 40-hour workweek itself reveals another truth: one of the things we do with higher wage rates is to enjoy the luxury of working less. A century ago, when average wages were far lower than they are today, the workweek extended to 60 hours and more. People had to work this long to earn enough to make ends meet. But, as increasing economic efficiency allowed average wages to climb (as workers' marginal revenue productivities increased), workers opted for less, rather than more work, and the 48-hour workweek and now the 48-hour workweek became normal.

This apparent contradiction of the law of supply results from our having to be present in person, while we supply our labor. Whether we know it or not, we are making those difficult, and yet ever-so-subjective cost-benefit analysis decisions. Leisure time has value, and so we equate the marginal utility of another hour of work with the marginal utility of another hour of leisure. The equilibrium is often elusive, since we probably could always use a little more money, but who among us would deny the value of a little free time for ourselves?

Besides, "all work and no play makes John (Jane) a dull boy (girl)." Not to take this human dimension into account would be not to think like an economist.

Chapter 11

THE ENVIRONMENT

> *The Moving Finger writes; and, having writ,*
> *Moves on: nor all your Piety nor Wit*
>   *Shall lure it back to cancel half a Line,*
> *Nor all your Tears wash out a Word of it.*
>
> – *Omar Khayyám (1050?-1123), Persian poet*

At first glance, it may seem as if this eleventh century passage from Omar Khayyám's *Rubáiyát* has little to do with either the environment or the economic way of thinking. In fact, most people today believe that many of our worst environmental crises–pollution and environmental exhaustion–are the result of greed, stupidity, and irresponsibility, or at least the result of a remarkably inconsiderate and shortsighted profit motive. These factors certainly contribute, of course, and so it's understandable that our environmental protection policies focus directly on these failings. The good news is that we can and do use economic incentives to influence people's short run behavior. The bad news is that, in long run, the ultimate root of the problem runs deeper.

Time Out For A Brief Physics Lesson

Environmental problems cannot ever go completely away, because they are caused by the immutable law of physics called the second law of thermodynamics, also known as the law of entropy. This law states that any and all actions in the universe are driven by the dispersal of higher energy concentrations into the lower energy ambiance of the surrounding environment. That is, a steam engine can generate power to the degree that its steam is hotter than the surrounding air into which it escapes. If either the surrounding air were as hot as the engine's steam or the steam were as cold as the surrounding air, the engine couldn't move a piston.

The law of entropy applies not only to steam engines or other mechanical devices, it applies to all animate and inanimate actions and events. Every beat of our hearts, every bloom of a flower, every crash of breaking surf, and every puff of summer breeze "consumes" energy, in the sense that higher energy disappears into the ambient surrounds. Any attempt to regroup this energy into a useful, higher concentration again only consumes still more energy. So, in effect, the law of entropy dictates that our universe runs relentlessly on a one-way street towards the complete exhaustion of all useful energies, i.e. the state of final entropy.

But not to worry! While our mountains will surely erode into the global oceans and our Earth will be consumed by a cooling and expanding Sun, our solar system will lose its spin, and the entire universe will turn into a thin soup of undifferentiated, homogenized space, this thermodynamic apocalypse won't happen in our lifetimes, nor in a thousand-times-a-thousand lifetimes. As such, the final consequences of the law of entropy are of little concern to us. What *is* important is that the law operates just as relentlessly in the microcosms of the universe that make up our daily lives. It operates everywhere, in everything, and at all times, including our factories, farms, and businesses, our nations and our homes.

Pollution and Resource Exhaustion

Pollution and resource exhaustion are our two main environmental problems. Many others, such as species extinctions, possible global warming, and urban noise and congestion, can be seen as aspects of these larger problems. Pollution is the befouling and defiling of some part of the air, water, and/or land in our environment. Specifically, it is smog, chemical spills, dumped garbage, and so on. Resource exhaustion is the using up of a once valuable natural asset, such as the depletion of the iron ore in the Mesabi Range, the redwood trees in California, the water table in the

Chapter 11: The Environment

Edwards aquifer in Texas, and so on. For analytical purposes–and to be realistic about it–we can often regard pollution and resource exhaustion as the same problem seen from different angles. For example, smog is the exhaustion of the capacity of a region's air to remain clean and fresh. The defilement of our nation's scenic highways, beaches, and rivers can all be thought of in the same way.

Yet, in spite of the aforementioned prevalence and persistence of human greed, stupidity, and irresponsibility, neither pollution nor resource exhaustion are ever likely to be the intended primary outcome of an activity. Making something dirty or causing something to become used up, as ends in themselves, are hardly likely to be rewarding activities. Instead, they are the byproducts, the intentional (and sometimes unintentional) side effects of other purposeful behaviors.

That is, we don't chop vegetables in the kitchen to make garbage. We chop them to make dinner. For this reason, these side effects have traditionally been considered to be outside of the context of decision making concerns. The kitchen garbage–just like the factory smoke, the mine acids flowing into nearby creeks and streams, the gradually disappearing top soils of midwestern farms, and so on–may be regrettable, but it is external to the decision calculus determining whether or not and to what degree chopping vegetables is worthwhile doing.

Ages ago, when we humans lived in primitive economies–think of our cave dwelling ancestors or even the teepee dwelling Native Americans of more recent times–there were very few people and an apparently limitless countryside. Garbage was no problem. Neither was resource exhaustion. When the campgrounds began to smell too bad of various wastes, when much of the local game had been hunted and killed, when plant and human pathogens had begun to zero in on the crops and the people, the tribe picked up stakes and moved to new ground.

The last such major move was the emigration of populations to the relatively sparsely populated continents of the Americas, Africa, and Australia, in recent centuries. The next one, according to some not necessarily crazy astrophysicists, is a move to colonies in outer space. In any case, the Planet Earth is seen as a finite globe now, and the countryside is no longer perceived as limitless. The time has come to become concerned about the kitchen garbage, so to speak.

The Incentive To Pollute

Pollution doesn't just happen, it happens because there is an incentive to pollute. Usually, it happens because it is "the easy way out," or the lowest cost alternative from among a range of alternative actions. For example, for centuries factories located alongside rivers and streams. In part, this was because the moving water served as a source of energy. Also, if big enough, the river provided the transportation for both raw materials and finished products. Just as importantly, however, the moving water served as a disposal mechanism for the effluents, or the garbage, produced by the factory.

When it wasn't feasible to locate along rivers, factories were often built with tall smokestacks so that the garbage could be discharged high above the city, in hopes that prevailing winds would disperse the pollutants before they fell on the people below. Other factories simply dug huge pits and deposited their wastes–some quite toxic it turns out–and covered them with topsoil and shrubbery. Some toxic waste sites, such as the Love Canal, were even turned into residential home sites where people lived . . . and children died.

In any case, factories that dump their garbage into the rivers, the atmosphere, and the soil–as well as the primitive nomadic tribes that moved from one location to another–all have something in common. All ended up lowering their cost of production by using the environment as a giant waste disposal system. And, in a market economy where lower costs of production normally translate into higher profits for producers, pollution (on behalf of the polluters) may even make sense. The result, then, is that producers have an economic incentive to pollute–something which is very much of a problem when we are the ones who have to deal with their garbage.

Internalizing The External Costs

Economists like to think of pollution as a *negative externality,* a kind of economic side effect that harms a third party not directly involved in the activity that caused it. These negative externalities are actually a cost to innocent third parties–as when we have to pay additional medical bills to cover the treatment of respiratory problems caused by pollution or as when we take the time to pick up fast food wrappers and beer cans which find their way to our front lawns.

The trick is to identify those costs that fall on others and then shift them back to the persons, businesses, or governments that created them in the first place. After all, if all of the people who throw trash out of their car windows, along with all of the firms that discharge wastes into the air or water, along with all of the government agencies such as the military who exclude their fleets of trucks and transport vehicles from air quality standards, could be made to pay for cleaning up the messes they make, pollution would be much abated.

This is hardly feasible in most cases, as in the instance of people who pitch litter out the window of their vehicles, and so state and local governments have responded by posting signs announcing minor fines for littering in hopes that it will deter this behavior. In other situations, as in the case of auto emissions, the federal government has decreed the use of catalytic converters and even cleaner mixtures of oxygenated gas in order to reduce auto emissions. In even other situations, such as the control of sulfur emissions from power plants, some solutions have been quite clever.

In 1993, for example, the Environmental Protection Agency (EPA) instituted a program using pollution permits in an effort to reduce sulfur dioxide emissions–a key component of acid rain. Each permit allowed a public utility to release one ton of sulfur dioxide in the air as electricity was generated. The permits were auctioned at the Chicago Board of Trade, and each permit initially cost the utilities several hundred dollars each. Over time, the EPA planned to auction fewer permits than in the previous year, which would cause the price of each permit to rise. The increasing cost of the permits would then encourage the utilities to design more efficient methods of production or to install additional anti-pollution devices.

This technique is called internalizing the costs, or making the polluter pick up the tab, thereby suffering increased costs. As painful as this may be to the "internee," it generates three major positive results for the economy. One is that it lifts the burden of the costs off the shoulders of the innocent third parties. The utilities may argue that the cost of pollution permits drives up the cost of electricity for consumers, but the utilities' customers are not the innocent third parties in this case–they are the direct users of the energy supplied by the utilities, and the very ones who should pay for all of the costs of producing electricity. The higher prices that the customers pay simply reflect the costs of reducing the pollution.

The second major positive result is that, by creating a more realistic accounting of all the costs involved, it reduces the amount of the environmentally injurious behavior. That is, the higher prices the customers now pay for electricity, to continue that example, also encourages them to turn off the lights, when they are not needed, and to go easy on the air conditioning. By saving money this way, they reduce the pollution caused by the electricity generating station.

Third, and finally, the process of internalizing costs actually conserves resources. When consumers are forced to pay a larger–and more equitable–share of the true cost of generating electricity, they are naturally more conscious of the way they use it, and will probably use less electricity in the long run (remember the law of demand states that, at higher prices, less of a product will be demanded), thereby slowing the rate of resource exhaustion.

So while we may not always like the higher prices we pay when costs are internalized, there is a compelling logic to having the people who use certain products pay for the full cost of producing them. Besides, this reduces the burden on innocent third parties, reduces pollution, and conserves resources. Not bad at all!

Theoretically, we could even apply this logic to reducing other forms of pollution, such as the timely removal of the advertising posters described in Chapter 4, page 23. If a one dollar "disposal fee" is levied to cover the cost of removing and discarding (recycling?) every poster printed, the cost of each would double. At two dollars per poster, the entire $10 promotional budget would probably have gone to giving away free product samples, because the incremental return on the first poster, the one with the highest marginal revenue returns, would be less than the marginal returns on the last free sample.

If Only Everything Were That Easy!

So, with innocent third parties no longer having to bear the brunt of someone else's contra-environmental behavior, and with the true costs–including the environmental costs–of all activities being accounted and paid for by the perpetrators, our environmental problems should be on the way to being resolved once and for all. Obviously, they aren't.

One reason is that such a complete accounting and attribution of all costs is very difficult to achieve and very difficult to enforce. Even when all the resources involved and all the assets affected are clearly somebody's property and have a readily available price tag, it is often difficult to impose a complete and thorough accounting and attribution of costs. If the dandelion seeds from my neighbor's grungy back yard blow onto my immaculate, showpiece front lawn, I will have a hard time convincing that neighbor to pay the cost of spreading weed killer on my lawn to kill the invading dandelions. Indeed, from the perspective of economic analysis–if not necessarily from the perspective of ethics and justice–an equally efficient way to resolve the problem would be for me to pay for a 2-4-D treatment on the neighbor's yard that would kill all his dandelions. (I'd sooner treat it with Agent Orange!)

The difficulty is even greater when some of the resources and assets are not owned by anyone and, thus, have no price tag. Most of the cod, haddock, and halibut will have been fished to depletion in North Atlantic waters in another few years, terminating a centuries old fishing industry, because neither the fish nor the waters they are caught in are owned by anyone (or by any business, agency, or political entity). When something isn't owned, no one has jurisdiction to manage it. And the fishing fleets, coming from several different nations and being quite unorganized, see the end of their livelihoods drawing close. So, there is nothing for these fishermen to do with their fishing fleets, but to race each other for the last available fish, which guarantees a quick and, perhaps, permanent end to both their industry and to these species of fish.

The other reason our environmental problems are not resolved is spelled out in the beginning of this chapter: everything that happens in this universe consumes usable energy, which is to say that everything that happens in this universe changes the environment in which it happens. Our world is the way it is today, because of all the changes wrought by the law of entropy, since the beginning of time. And it will be a different world again tomorrow, for the same reason. Indeed, the pace of change increases as the number and the magnitude of activities and events increases. Our economic behavior is a very large and rapidly growing contributor to all these activities and events. A steel mill or a lumbering operation may not change the landscape as fast as, let's say, a major Mt. St. Helens-sized volcanic eruption, but there are more steel mills and lumbering operations than there have been major volcanic eruptions. So, ironically, the more productive our industry and agriculture becomes, the more rapidly our economy grows, the more surely we undermine the very environment that made these successes possible.

Our only response to this ever changing reality is to roll with it. Environmental change not only destroys some resources and opportunities, it also uncovers new ones. All of the species of plants and animals alive on the earth today–and that is less than half of all those that have ever lived–owe their existence to having been able to take advantage of new conditions. Those whose survival is now threatened, such as the cheetah or the gorilla, are endangered because they are unable to adapt to changed environments. Let's hope that we Homo Sapiens are unlikely to become endangered this way; we do seem to be among the most adaptable of species, along with house flies, crab grass, and cold germs. But all of us know of businesses, labor unions, farms, social and religious organizations, families, and even whole nations that have gone under or are going under, because they couldn't or can't find new opportunities in a changed environment.

Thinking Like A (Modern) Economist

Economists were slow to accept the centrality of the law of entropy to our lives. By categorizing environmental considerations as externalities, they tended to place these concerns outside of the mainstream of economic science. None of the early, most renowned economists, not Adam Smith, John Stuart Mill, David Ricardo, Alfred

Marshall, Karl Marx, nor John Maynard Keynes had much to say about environmental economics.

Indeed, the most conventional textbook diagram of a functioning economy, still used today and shown below, presents us with an impossible, nineteenth century perpetual motion machine, in which money and goods flow endlessly around and around between households and businesses in an unchanging economy.

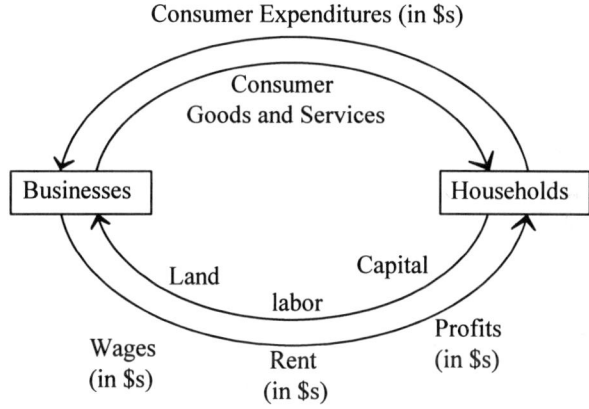

Yet, as useful as the above diagram is to illustrate how the circular flow of money expenditures and wages mirrors the flow of real goods and labor, and how these flows may be momentarily equal, it also misleadingly implies that such flows can be perpetual. Nothing can be further from the truth.

A more realistic way of thinking about the economy is to see it as a sequence of transformations moving through time and towards increasing entropy, as shown below. Production leads to consumption. That is obvious—we can't consume anything unless we have made it available to ourselves by some kind of production process. But consumption is also necessary for production to proceed, because—to put it in its simplest context—if we don't eat, we die. Abundant and effective consumption results in health and

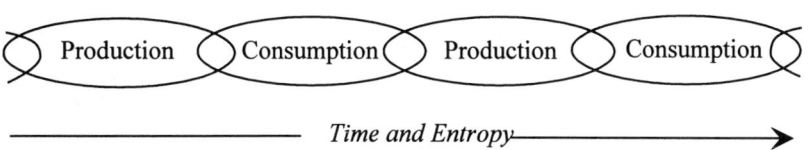

vigorous people, who, in turn, become vigorous and efficient producers.

So the chain is linked together: production leads to consumption, and consumption leads to production. There is no first link and no last. But it's not a circular process. With each new link, the world is changed. Resources are used up, pollutants are generated, entropy is advanced. Yet, as long as new opportunities are available and we are able to take advantage of them, the chain continues.

It still probably comes as a great disillusionment to those of us who had hoped that we may someday live in a pollution free and permanently sustainable environment, that it can never happen. If greed, stupidity, and irresponsibility–all the perceived causes of environmental mischief–were the only causes of our pollution and environmental exhaustion, our problems might conceivably have been solvable, even though these unattractive human traits are all too normal and all too persistent. In the end, however, they are not the ultimate root of the problems.

Chapter 12

POVERTY

Understanding a problem is half its solution.
-Anonymous

A substantial majority of all Americans–including both the authors and readers of this book–identify ourselves as middle class. This includes some of us who are very well off, as well as some who are barely scraping by. Being so all-inclusive, membership in the middle class would hardly seem to be a significant distinction, and for many purposes, including sociological analyses and market researchers, the middle class–with all of its fuzzy boundaries–is hardly a useful concept. Much finer distinctions, such as categorizing people by income, age, sex, size of household, geographical location, race, or even such popular stereotypings as yuppies and twinkies (young, upwardly mobile professionals and two incomes, no kids) can be much more revealing–so why is the concept of the so-called "middle class" so important?

The Mainstream

Roughly speaking, the middle class defines the socioeconomic position between the lower working classes and the wealthy. That may not seem like a very precise definition, but it helps position the middle class as that giant mainstream in our society which exercises so much purposeful economic behavior. In fact, this is one of the defining characteristics of the middle class: in greater or lesser degree, members of the middle class have the freedom, the ability, and suffer the necessity of having to manage income and expenditures. Obviously, this describes most of us, and that is why the vast majority of us consider ourselves middle class. The really poor have nothing to manage. The really rich hardly need to manage.

Through most of human history significant segments of many populations were exempt from economically productive activities, by virtue of having aristocratic wealth and income, or by pursuing the other-worldly goals of the clergy, or even the predatory goals of the military. The largest exempt group, however, were always the poor: the slaves, the serfs, the landless peasants, the beggars, and the vagabonds. They could do very little in life to improve their lot. And, they were so numerous at times that they were considered "the common man," the "blessed . . . poor," who will inherit the earth.

The problem is that economic progress is a virtual impossibility whenever people live so close to subsistence. Whatever meager resources people have are consumed by the day-to-day struggle for survival–leaving little, if any, surplus to be managed in a productive manner. Even today, such a socioeconomic scenario from antiquity or the middle ages would seem familiar in the poorest, most undeveloped economies of the world.

The Emerging Middle Class

Economic development changes all that. Industrialization, the commercialization of agriculture, technological advances, and, above all, the development of markets and trade require large numbers of people to pursue all this economically productive activity. It was, in fact, this very industrialization over the last several centuries that provided the spawning ground for the ubiquitous and overwhelming middle class. Writing in the middle of the eighteen hundreds in England, when and where this economic development was proceeding at an unprecedented pace, Karl Marx identified the capitalist owners of the new industrial and commercial enterprises exclusively as the new ruling middle class or, in his word, the bourgeoisie.

Class distinctions were a useful pedagogical tool, but Marx generally failed to see that the workers in these developing economies, by eventually bringing their capital assets in the form of acquired productive skills and experience to their jobs, would also become capitalists of a sort and would also begin to identify themselves as middle class. As a result, the class war that he predicted between the bourgeoisie and the proletariat–the communist revolution between the capitalists and the workers–never happened. Instead, the middle class just grew and became more inclusive.

Even many of the very rich were part of the great middle class at one time or another. Think of Bill Gates and Ross Perot or, earlier, John D. Rockefeller and Andrew Carnegie. All worked very hard for their money, and most used their surplus to enhance the economic progress of their business interests. How different they are and were from, let's say, a typical rich medieval French aristocrat or an Indian maharajah, neither of whom ever lifted a productive finger. There are also still those who aren't necessarily rich, but who exempt themselves from productive economic activity by virtue of their religious, counter-cultural, or military purposes in life.

And then there are the poor, the unfortunates at the very bottom of the socioeconomic spectrum.

Defining Poverty

To be poor is to be in poverty, which is, of course, a relative term. Country folk can often live better on low incomes than those living in the city, and some of the poor in the United States would seem quite well off in other, less developed countries. In order to standardize the American definition of poverty, the U.S. Social Security Administration developed poverty threshold measures back in 1964 which in turn were based on two studies done by the Department of Agriculture in the 1950s. The first study by the USDA developed four nutritionally adequate, but alternative food plans for individuals and families. The least expensive food plan was then selected as the one that would keep people out of poverty.

The second study conducted by the USDA found that families typically spend a third of their total budget on food. So, if the least expensive food budget for a family of a given size was $4,000, and if this represents one-third of the typical total budget, then the poverty threshold would be defined as $12,000. This number is then adjusted for single individuals and families of different sizes. Also, slightly higher rates are used for Alaska and Hawaii.

Finally, the poverty threshold is indexed every year so that it increases at the same rate as inflation. To illustrate, a nonfarm family of four, according to one of these tables, was considered officially poor if its annual income was $8,414 or less in 1980, $13,359 in 1990, and $15,600 in 1996.

Poverty, thus defined, seems to be shrinking slowly over the long run in America. Over 22 percent of all Americans lived in poverty 1960, while more recent numbers are in the 14-15 percent range. Short run changes may be caused by adjustments in the way poverty limits are defined, adjustments in the way statistical data is collected, and by the currently prevailing state of the economy.

Always of particular concern, however, are the poverty rates of children, which are frighteningly high. From 1990-94 the average for all children in America was slightly over 20 percent. This exceeded 50 percent in single parent families (regardless of race), and surpassed 65 percent in single parent African American or Hispanic families. If ever there were people likely to be excluded from the mainstream middle class in America, these children are the prime candidates.

A Recipe For Poverty

Like accidents, poverty in America doesn't just happen; it is caused. Imagine a person who is

>unskilled,
>uneducated,
>illiterate or, at best, a slow reader,
>not able to do simple arithmetic,
>inarticulate in English,
>socially inept,
>physically unfit,
>unhealthy or HIV positive,
>unattractive to look at,
>alcoholic or addicted to drugs,
>unconnected to a functioning family,

in past or present trouble with the law,
very young or very old,
physically or mentally handicapped, and
a member of a group victimized by bigotry,

and we will almost certainly see a person locked in the grip of poverty. Furthermore, as long as the above list seems, any one of us could probably add a few more itemized causes of poverty. And, as if to make matters worse, a few or maybe even just one of the items on the list above–such as alcoholism or illiteracy–can do the trick, can make a person poor.

Can Poverty Be Prevented?

Notice that almost all the causes of poverty, except the last three on the list, are largely preventable by the potentially poor person him- or herself. That is, we can learn some skills, get educated, improve our reading and arithmetic, work on speaking better, develop our social graces, attend to our health and appearance, stay away from booze and drugs, and become law abiding citizens. Again, we may not have to do all of these things. A few fixes here and there, such a learning how to read and write or picking up a marketable skill, may help us to escape the potential grip of poverty.

So we may be tempted to blame the poor themselves for their poverty: "If only they could get their acts together, they wouldn't be so poor!" To be sure, many poor do get their acts together and climb out of their poverty successfully. But this explanation is an oversimplification. First of all, just a few or even just one cause of poverty can precipitate more causes of poverty, which together close the poverty trap tightly. In the above mentioned example, alcoholism or illiteracy can prevent a person from understanding the warnings about behavior that leads to HIV infection. Once a person is HIV positive, on top of being alcoholic or illiterate or both, the trap is beginning to snap shut, and poverty is becoming a terminal condition.

Secondly, people who are very young or very old, physically or mentally handicapped, and/or the victims of bigotry are essentially powerless to do much about them. Only help from the outside can lighten their burden.

American society seems to have been quite forthcoming with help for the young, the old, and the handicapped from its very beginning. The early settlers and pioneers cultivated strong families and responsible communities that tended to take care of their own orphans, incompetent old people, the handicapped–including the proverbial village idiot–and other unfortunates. Even today, charity appeals and volunteer work, including everything from Meals on Wheels and foster parentage to our big national fund raising efforts for cancer research, Special Olympics, and many other good causes, play a larger role in American life than in almost any other nation in the world.

In the past several decades, our government has passed several civil rights and equal employment opportunity laws intended to redress the injustices created by bigotry, and to assure equal access for those formerly excluded by bigotry and/or being handicapped. Officially, at least, America is eager to ease the burdens created by the last three items of the list. Change is often painful, however, and some individuals, some social groups, and even a few state and local governments have resisted these progressive efforts–although the resistance is usually, and eventually, overcome.

Still, being very young or old, physically or mentally handicapped, and/or a victim of bigotry remain powerful ingredients in the recipe for poverty, in spite of all our best intentions. The problem persists largely because of those two undermining adjectives in the paragraph above: *"usually"* and *"eventually."* If only they were *always* and *immediately*, instead! But bigotry is an attitude as old as envy and hatred. Furthermore, the last-hope social safety nets provided by public and private agencies are patchy screens that let many victims fall through. And compounding all these problems, as always, is that these last three ingredients in the poverty recipe work synergistically with each other and with all the rest of the ingredients. For example, take a pinch of bigotry, add the bad education provided by ghetto schools, toss in a very young age and very little or no family support, and the poverty trap is once again practically inescapable.

The final reason why poverty can be an inescapable trap is that some of our most well intended antipoverty programs actually exacerbate some of the otherwise preventable causes of poverty on the list. The most conspicuous example of this is the Aid to Families with Dependent Children program, which discouraged the establishment and cultivation of traditional two-parents-with-kids households, thus tightening the grip of the poverty trap. The resulting welfare dependency of the poor has become a major social and political issue in America, certainly generating more heat than light.

The rationality of accepting welfare and eventually becoming dependent on it often escapes the understanding of the people in the mainstream middle class, who have so many preferable alternatives in their own lives. The main defining characteristic of poverty, however, is that it is not in the American mainstream. This means that the normal abundance of opportunities–opportunities in our education, where we live, who our friends are, where we can find work, and so on–are very drastically restricted in the lives of the poor. Welfare, even welfare dependency, given the dearth of alternatives, can be a perfectly rational choice, under these circumstances.

Thinking Like An Economist

And so we've come back to our original emphasis on understanding poverty in America as being caused by the exclusion of some unfortunate individuals–those who will be subsequently identified as the "poor"–from the otherwise very widely inclusive middle class. This clears up an important misconception about poverty: that it is created by the better-off members of society exploiting the poor, cruelly taking advantage of their weakness and vulnerability. Of course, in the harsh reality of our world, there are, indeed, rapacious landlords, cheating merchants, fraudulent lawyers, quack doctors, drug pushers, con artists, and all that beastly menagerie who find the ignorant and entrapped as easy prey. They take advantage of the poor, but they aren't a primary cause of poverty.

In fact, poor people, being poor, are not good prospects for any significant kind of exploitation. Quite the contrary: the middle class tries in every way it can to insulate and isolate itself from the poor. It moves out of poor neighborhoods, takes its children out of schools that have too many pupils from poor homes, dislikes shopping in poor districts of the city, avoids hospitals that serve a disproportionate number of poor people, refuses to lend mortgage money to people buying real estate in "redlined" poor sections of town, and so on. It's as if the poor lived in another country . . . or even another planet.

Conventional wisdom has it that "understanding a problem is half its solution." Many of the causes of poverty are easy enough to understand. Yet they are often deeply anchored in the texture of American society, and solving them will not be easy. Furthermore, many of these causes of poverty, such as age, physical or mental deprivation, or bigotry, may not be primarily economic problems, so they won't submit to primarily economic solutions.

Solving the problem of poverty, then, is not just accomplished by economic development. To be sure, this is the first prerequisite, and "a rising tide raises all boats." But it does so only if the boats are admitted to the economic swim of things. To recognize that exclusion from the mainstream of economic activity is at the root of our poverty in America today is to embrace the economic way of thinking about the problem–and to begin to find its solution.

Chapter 13

THE ECONOMICS OF CRIME

> *If you do big things they print your face, and if you do little things they print only your thumbs.*
> – Arthur "Bugs" Baer (1886-1969), American journalist

With mainstream, middle class America being so far out of reach of the poor, it is easy to assume that the poor might rationally turn to non-mainstream, illegal, and criminal opportunities to support themselves. Many social analysts and concerned citizens claim to have found powerful connections between being poor and being criminal. But an explanation of crime primarily as a response to poverty may be too easy by half. Criminal behavior cuts across all socioeconomic boundaries, and, just as there are many absolutely honest-but-poor people in this world, there is also a rather significant number of well-off criminals. However, there are similarities between crime and poverty, and they have to do with exclusion from that great mainstream, the middle class in America today. This is the fundamental understanding on which our economic analysis is built.

The Nature of Crime

Economists like to distinguish between crimes that have victims and those don't have victims. The former would include assault, murder, rape, arson, burglary, theft, mugging, car jacking, and all those illegal acts in which a victim or victims suffer damages. Notice that many of these crimes–the first four on the above list, for example–seem to be purely crimes of insanity, passion, and irrationality. No one benefits from them in any normal way, not the perpetrator of the crime and certainly not the victim. They are generally first understood as expressions of anger, perverse lust, macho status seeking, thrill seeking, or even as impulsive behavioral mistakes. Some of these overruling passions also seem to play a role in the more rational crimes–the last four on the above list, for example–adding quite some spice to the sober analysis with which we may try to understand these acts.

In any case, over the years, our national crime statistics have tended to correlate positively with the growing or the waning of that proportion of our population that is young, and youth is an age both for passions and for mistakes. Yet, it helps to understand that many of these crimes, even those primarily motivated by thrills, hate, anger, misdirected testosterone, or whatever other perversity, are a not entirely irrational response to being an outsider, to being excluded from the mainstream middle class. Lacking the abundance of legitimate expressive and productive opportunities–and opportunities to make mistakes–regularly available to the members of the middle class, these outsiders turn to criminal opportunities.

When Crime Pays

Economists like to evaluate every opportunity, from new business ventures and government projects to investments in stocks and bonds to consumer purchases and so on, in terms of the probable costs and the probable benefits this opportunity will create. For example, if an opportunity has, let's say, an eighty percent probability of earning $1,000 worth of beneficial returns for us each time we take this opportunity, and a twenty percent probability of creating $1,000 worth of some kind of losses to us, its probable net benefit to us over the long run is $.8(\$1,000) + .2(-\$1,000) = \$600$ worth of benefits. Admittedly, this very simple analysis says nothing about how an individual event will turn out; we also can't very well predict whether a single flip of a coin will turn heads or tails. In the long run, however, this kind of analysis is a good estimator, just as we predict fifty percent heads and fifty percent tails more and more accurately, as the number of times we flip a coin increases.

The use of such cost-benefit analyses that uses outcomes based on probabilities–strategies sometimes also described as decision analyses or risk analyses–have become very sophisticated in recent years. A whole new field of specialization and a new consulting industry providing this service to industry and government have evolved. New testing technologies, mathematics, and computer programs have been developed, and the analyses have been extended to include societal and environmental considerations as well, mostly in response to new governmental regulations and requirements. But the ultimate purpose of all cost-benefit analyses, whether carried out simply and quickly by an individual facing a choice or undertaken in full dress by a large corporation or government agency, is to determine whether taking an opportunity is worthwhile or not.

Some criminal acts can be subjected to the same analyses. A burglary that nets, let's say, $1,000 in cash, with only a twenty percent chance of getting caught, would seem like a good bet, but only if the cost–twenty percent times its incurred loss (fines, jail time, or both)–is comfortably less than the benefit–eighty percent times $1,000. To those who argue that criminals are not likely to engage in such businesslike cost-benefit analyses, we can reply that experience seems to prove that two fundamental ways of encouraging crime are to lower the odds on getting caught and, if the criminal is caught, to reduce the penalty.

Another fundamental encouragement to crime is to increase the probable benefits payoff or, at least, to make the probable benefits payoff bigger than that which any of the other available opportunities can offer. For people outside of America's middle class, the qualifying threshold for such opportunities can be quite low. Even a convenience store stickup yielding only $37.23 may seem worthwhile, when no other alternatives are as available. Again, not being in the middle class, and therefore not having a range of attractive alternatives from which to choose, is at the core of the problem.

A Bad Situation Can Get Worse

The problem is compounded when crime is driven by substance abuse, especially the use of common street drugs like heroin, cocaine, or any of the new designer drugs that pop up from time to time.

While the proceeds from a convenience store stickup would seem almost trivial to those of us in the great middle class, it may be a matter of utmost urgency to the perpetrator. To make matters worse, the perpetrator may need to resort to crime again and again to satisfy the needs of the addiction.

A person with a substance abuse addiction has a highly inelastic demand for the product–a demand characterized by the inability to delay consumption and the lack of adequate substitutes. Depending on the extent of the addiction, price may not even be a factor in the decision to consume. As a result, attempts by law enforcement agencies to reduce the availability of an illegal street drug by interdicting supply generally tends to raise the street price of the drug and the profits of the drug distributors. As far as the addict is concerned, he or she will still need the next fix and so will turn to shoplifting, mugging, robbery, or whatever to finance the next purchase. Indeed, some experts have argued that such a scenario may actually increase the rate of crime.

Finally, many of the economically disenfranchised and hard-core teenage criminals in our inner cities have grown up in a hardened street culture climate. These individuals are so far removed from the middle class that they may never even want to change behaviors, even if they were able to do so. Indeed, the peer group and other social pressures to keep up with the demands of the street culture–the need for drugs, exaggerated masculinity and sexual prowess–are so far removed from the values of the great middle class that the costs and benefits received by these individuals are almost beyond imagining.

Victimless Crimes

The rationale for victimless crimes is a bit different. Selling sex, or growing marijuana, gambling, and distilling whiskey at home–the list goes on–all involve willing participants, none of whom want to get caught and none of whom are likely to call the cops. If it weren't for our perception that prostitution, pot farming, poker parties, and so on were all antisocial or even immoral behaviors, we would be hard pressed to find the crime in them. Indeed, more than a few economists argue that some of these crimes should be redefined as legitimate enterprises, in which case a substantial part of our crime statistics would simply be transformed into entries in our legitimate Gross Domestic Product accounts.

Victimless crimes seem to be especially appealing opportunities for formal criminal organizations. Perhaps because they supply desired goods and services similarly to the way legitimate businesses do, they also tend to resemble the organizational structure of legitimate businesses. And it is not surprising that successful Mafia operatives may eventually opt to "go straight," by investing their criminal profits and entrepreneurial talents in legitimate businesses and disappearing into the great mainstream middle class. As always, when a progressive, robust, and inclusive middle class has better opportunities to offer, crime will diminish.

Of course, there may always be some people who prefer to do what they are not supposed to do.

Thinking Like an Economist

We do not in any way diminish our many other social problems, such as teenage pregnancy, high divorce rates, poor schools, overburdened courts, or even the daily gridlock of rush hour traffic, by pointing out that crime and poverty are our two most serious social problems. Indeed, some of these other social problems are just different aspects of crime or poverty. What makes all these social problems so hard to understand and even harder to solve is that, as we have seen, they are often driven by bigotry, fear, anger, and other irrational motives. Even when the crime and the behavior of the poor are rational responses to real circumstances, the limitations suffered by people not in the middle class result in behavior that tends to reinforce their exclusion from the middle class, and the cycle is difficult to break.

Economists frequently throw up their hands and let others, such as sociologists, psychologists, case workers, and parole officers deal with crime and poverty. After all, economics, the quintessential science of rational behavior, would seem to them to have little to offer towards the understanding of such irrational and unbusinesslike phenomena. But, as we have seen in all of this and the foregoing chapter, crime and poverty do follow their own logic, especially when it is understood that criminals and the poor are exempted and/or excluded from mainstream middle class considerations and opportunities.

And so, the criminal elements among us are far more rational than is widely supposed. At first it may seem as if only few of our criminals bother (or even have the ability) to assess the probabilities of capture and conviction, or make the difficult and elusive cost-benefit calculations, establish priorities, and so on. But this is hardly the case. Clearly those who commit the majority of our white collar crimes, along with those who commit the majority of the victimless crimes, and even those who commit the $37.23 convenience store stickups, are well aware of the costs and benefits of their actions. These individuals simply have a different–and generally much more restricted–range of alternatives from which to choose.

Even those conspicuously irrational motives, such as the angers and lusts that drive the "senseless" crimes, seem a little less irrational when understood in this context. As Arthur "Bugs" Baer realized, you have to do big things to get your face printed, otherwise all you get is your thumbs.

Chapter 14

ECONOMIC SYSTEMS AND INSTITUTIONS

No man is an island.
– John Donne (1572-1631), English poet

When we come right down to it, businesses, management teams, political parties, government agencies, Boy Scout troops, the sets of parents of children–any and all kinds of groups of people–neither think nor make decisions. Only individual people do. Losing sight of this fundamental philosophic truth can lead to damaging miscalculations and has led to some terrifying immoralities.

When individuals such as you and I think and make decisions, we are almost never entirely alone, answerable only to ourselves. All of us exist in a variety of institutional relationships with other people that powerfully influence how we think and what we decide. There are thousands of such institutions. What distinguishes the economic ones from all the others is that economic institutions and systems are the instruments through which production and consumption are organized, ownership of property is recognized, and through which the transfer of this property–the movement of goods and services from one person to another–is realized. Here are the most important economic institutions and systems.

Families

A momma, a poppa, and a sonny and sis: the quintessential modern family has become such a paradigm of propriety, towards which even television sitcoms and campaigning politicians pretend to aspire, that we tend to forget that families have always taken many different shapes. From loosely knit clans to tightly held "until death do us part" monogamies, from large, multi-generational associations to small, single parent or married-couples-without-children twosomes, from marriages of political and/or economic convenience to rapturous romances, families have adjusted to the needs and opportunities of their particular times and places over the many thousands of years of human history. Today, families are being redefined so rapidly that official American statistics most often refer simply to households, rather than to families. It's probably convenient for us to think of families as households too.

What all functioning families–of whatever stripe–have always had in common, however, is that they are the vessels that contain much of our personal property–our land, our homes, our vehicles, our furniture and appliances, and our savings–and the vessels which pass this property on from family member to family member and to future generations. They are also the institutions which deliver the final product of the economic process to the individual consumer. Food, clothing, and shelter, as well as substantial portions of education, recreation, and all other consumer goods and services, are made available to individuals by their families. Of course, this is of critical importance to children, since human children cannot provide even the basic necessities of survival for themselves. So, in that way, families are also the critical institution for the very survival of the human race.

As critical as this is, families are yet much more. They establish the social identity and status of their members, the environment for personal and moral growth and well-being, and they provide the context for farsighted and responsible decision making. This last is an especially important economic concern. No other institution (read: persons acting within an institution) can entertain as long a decision horizon as a family, which takes into account not only the immediate outcome of a decision, like any acting organism; or the quarterly or annual outcome, like the manager of a corporation; or the outcome by next election, like a politician; but also the outcome ten or even fifty years down the road, for the children or the grandchildren. On a planet, such as ours, that is increasingly dominated by human behavior, where even the climate and the sea level will be influenced by our industrial and agricultural activity, the future is more and more in our own hands. Farsighted and responsible decisions are becoming increasingly important. Healthy, functioning families will be absolutely indispensable.

Families also provide for production. This may not be immediately obvious. For most of us, production, that is, working for a living, seems an individual undertaking often performed outside of the family. We have our individual jobs, our individual careers, and earn our own individual paychecks. The family comes into it–if we are living in a family household–only when we bring our income home to pay for the groceries, shoes, rent, and so on. However, a little introspection reveals that the purpose of our working for a living is to sustain our families, which, in turn, makes it possible for us to go to work every day, by providing us with the necessary food, clothing, shelter, and so on. As any householder knows, this is a full-time job to be performed either by a full-time person or, as is so often the case today, to be an added burden on the shoulders of those who already have a full-time job outside the home.

Proprietorships and Partnerships

The family is also frequently the nucleus around which businesses are formed. The prototypical business proprietorship or small farm is a family business. While these basic business institutions are usually owned, in the legal sense, by an individual proprietor or several partners, whole families are often actually involved. Husbands, wives, and children may all need to lend a hand. Children become assets, in these circumstances, rather than the expensive consumption goods they so often are in families where earning a living is more separated from family life.

Most of the almost twenty million business firms in America are proprietorships and partnerships. As we might expect, they are mostly small. Perhaps they are just starting out, or they are only part-time, or they are "Mom and Pop" operations. But they can become huge. The Ford Motor Company remained a proprietorship until 1946, and many multi-million dollar legal firms and investment brokerages are partnerships today. Of course, large or small, they all want to be profitable, that is, they all try to generate more revenues than costs. But for many–think of farms or restaurants that have been "in the family" for generations–these businesses represent a way of life, as much as a source of income and profits.

All of their assets–the farm land, the machinery, the shops, etc.–are owned by their proprietors or partners. All of their liabilities–the bank debts, the bills owed, etc.–are owed by the same. All of the revenues they earn and all the costs they incur add to and subtract from the proprietors' or partners' own finances. And, if the proprietors or partners have families, all of this applies to their families, as well. The risk that this imposes can be a powerfully deterring wet blanket on the businesses' enthusiasm for enterprise and growth. Furthermore, their net income, that is, total revenues minus total costs, is taxed as ordinary individual (read: family) income by the Internal Revenue Service.

In all of this, they often face two common problems. One is that proprietorships and partnerships can have many implicit, unaccounted-for assets, such as family owned land and buildings, many implicit resources, such as the labor contributed by unpaid family members, and many implicit costs and liabilities, such as family members dipping into the till occasionally. These can make it very difficult to ascertain the true financial conditions of these businesses. The other is that, when they have an opportunity to grow, they cannot easily raise more money for investment, without going into debt or without taking on another partner.

Corporations

So proprietorships and partnerships may be simple, but they are not always convenient. The solution to these problems is to incorporate. This makes separate legal entities, separate *corpuses*, out of these businesses, removing them from the legal responsibility of their proprietors or partners and their families. The businesses now own themselves, so to speak. Investors, including presumably the original proprietors or partners, but also including new people with new money to invest, own shares of the businesses. But the business liability of these share owners is limited to the amounts they invested, which is why corporations are commonly called "limiteds" in some countries. So two birds are killed with one stone: personal and family liability problems are solved, and new investors are encouraged to become share owners. As a result, businesses can grow, without anyone having to take out a second mortgage on the house or taking on an unwelcome brother-in-law as a new partner.

Since corporations are their own legal entities, their assets, liabilities, expenses, revenues, profits, and losses are likely to be much more explicitly and thoroughly accounted. All workers, including the bosses, are considered employees and are paid accordingly. The profits, measured as returns on investments, can be calculated more accurately and will be taxed as corporate profits by the Internal Revenue Service. The after-tax profits will either be reinvested in the businesses or will be distributed, as dividends, to share owners, where they will be taxed again as individual incomes.

These profits are likely to be perceived in a purely monetary way. This cold hearted and steely-eyed way of looking at the business of corporations is the source of much of the economic efficiency in modern free market economies today. The survival of even the largest corporations can be cruelly challenged by this one-dimensional calculus of profits, leading to what economist Joseph Schumpeter called "creative destruction," and resulting in powerful economic dynamism. Some shareholders protest such corporate policy at the annual meetings of their corporations, and some even choose to invest only in more broadminded and socially responsible corporations. But most share owners perceive little nonmonetary pleasure or pain from being associated with any particular corporation and, when it comes to deciding where to place their investment dollars, they just "go for the bucks."

So corporate businesses are almost entirely money-profits driven. The advantage is the clarity of their rationale. It becomes so objective and values-neutral that MBAs can study it as a management science. The disadvantage is that it become so objective and values-neutral.

The laws of incorporation differ somewhat from country to country and even from state to state in the United States, but corporations are the most important kinds of business organizations in the world today. Almost all big businesses are incorporated, and many small businesses have found it convenient to do so too. Perhaps surprisingly, then, corporations are a relatively new institutional invention, as business organizations go. The earliest ancestors of our modern corporations were probably the joint stock companies of the medieval European merchants, and the invention would have been stillborn without the development of double entry bookkeeping around the year 1500 AD, which allows ownership and indebtedness to be viewed from the standpoint of the business, rather than from the perspective of an individual.

Governments Again

By contrast, governments have existed since the dawn of civilization. As we saw in previous chapters, governments are powerful participants in the economy. One of the main uses to which the power, privilege, and initiative accruing to people in government is put, is to generate economic benefits for themselves, for their partisans and associates, and for all of the people they represent (in that order, cynics might say). In this regard, people in government behave very much like people in business. They want to do a good job, that is, they want to function effectively and efficiently; they want to succeed. In doing so, they generally follow the same disciplines and tactics as people in business.

However, there are two main differences between the goods and services production of governments and the goods and services production of businesses. The first is that government activity is not overtly profit driven. Most government provided goods and services do not even represent profit making opportunities. Consider two very large government undertakings: operating a military establishment and providing welfare for the poor. As important as these may be for the survival and well-being of a nation, neither of them suggest themselves as good opportunities for making money. And the second is that most government produced goods and services are produced for the "public good," rather than for sale to individual buyers. To cite the above examples again, we cannot individually arrange to buy as much or as little military defense against foreign aggression as we want, and welfare payments aren't something that can be bought or sold, at least, not legally.

These two differences often come to haunt government decision making and guarantee that government policies are always ripe for controversy. Even with the best and most businesslike intentions, when goods and services are not bought and sold, when they are not subject to the disciplines of the market, knowing what to produce and how much of it to produce becomes very difficult. And when profits are not at issue, when there is no "bottom line," identifying effectiveness and efficiency in production and being motivated to achieve them also become very difficult.

These two differences provide the economic rationale for conservatives' exhortation that "the government that governs least governs best." Yet, as was pointed out before, governments have a tendency to grow. Reaching out to larger constituencies, offering new goods and services, enlarging their budgets, expanding their buildings and grounds, adding personnel to their staffs, and acquiring more equipment–and especially technologically advanced equipment at that–is a familiar way of life for almost all bureaucracies. These are their measures of success, the sources of their prestige and power. In those countries that had been communist, government enterprise was almost the only economic game to play.

Central Planning

Most of these communist regimes went out of business in the last few decades of the twentieth century. They failed for many social and political reasons, but the economic reasons for their failures were certainly the most important. After World War II, while the United States and Western Europe experienced their most rapid economic growth on record, while the Asian "Tigers" and especially Japan become internationally competitive in the quality and quantity of their goods and services, and while many of the so-called third world countries joined the ranks of the "NICs" (the newly industrialized countries), the Soviet Union and its eastern European satellites gradually became economically strangled by their inefficient and limiting central planning.

Not that there is anything wrong with economic planning! We all do it, if we have any sense. Workers should plan their careers; families should plan for their children's education; businesses may plan for a new expansion or how to deal with an onslaught of new competition; and many large corporations have elaborate one, five, and ten year plans that rival those of national governments. But what economists mean by the term, central planning, is the replacement of most of these individual plans and decisions by government edicts. The result is an economy driven by the commands of a central governmental planning agency, rather than by the enterprise of free people responding voluntarily to market forces and opportunities and to their own self-interest.

Of course, government rules and regulations are nothing new. The mercantilist governments of the European nations throughout the seventeenth and eighteenth centuries regulated production and trade very strictly. So much so, in the case of England, that the American colonies fought a war to be free. However, a full-fledged, ideologically justified, peppercorns-to-shoelaces centrally planned national command economy was first attempted by the Soviet Union in the early part of the twentieth century. After several false starts and more than a few disasters, it chalked up some impressive economic successes, among them the development of a large steel industry, widespread electrification, universal education, and an armaments industry that, together with substantial help from the USA, successfully turned back the Nazi invasion in World War II.

Some of the egregious excesses of free market capitalism were avoided too. Totalitarian control made it possible to suppress private crimes (but set the scene for some horrifying government crimes). The tasteless antics of super-rich entertainment and sports personalities were avoided. And unemployment was, at least, officially eliminated, although Poland's Solidarity leader, Lech Walesa, spoke for many of the workers, when he said, "We pretend to work, and they pretend to pay us."

A major economic problem for communist central planning was that, in order to gain the power to implement such plans, all productive assets had to be controlled by the central planning agency. This meant that almost all the lands, buildings, machinery and equipment, underground resources–almost everything–became the property of the state or became rigidly regulated by the state. In addition to being an important justification for the inhuman totalitarianism that accompanies communism, such state ownership deprives individuals and their families of one of the main motives for energetic and effective economic activity: the promise of increasing personal and family property, the possibility of acquiring wealth. And nothing can squelch the urgency to use productive assets effectively and efficiently more that making such efforts irrelevant to anyone's personal and family prosperity.

After about sixty years, the Marxist-Leninist communist experiment was obviously unraveling. It may have been possible for the central planning agency to control the production of basic steel, electricity, and machinery, but it was not possible to command efficiency in production, to stimulate a spirit of enterprise, or to develop the wealth of consumer goods demanded of an advanced, modern economy. Agriculture, one of the most technologically sophisticated industries in modern free market economies, was notoriously backward. And one opportunity for progress after another, from cheap ballpoint pens to transistorized electronics, was missed. The eastern European satellite nations began to slip away, and, by 1991, the Soviet Union dissolved and became the Commonwealth of Independent States, most of which seem bent on flaunting their new independence by developing internationally competitive free market economies for themselves. It won't be easy, and some may not even make it, at least the first time around.

Some observers argue that, by the turn of the twentieth century, the very idea of a viable, centrally planned, command economy will be dismissed as impossible. Certainly we may hope that the world will never again have to suffer another repressive totalitarian regime like the major communist regimes of the twentieth century. But dissatisfaction with the materialism, individualistic profit seeking, and moral neutrality–not to say amorality–sometimes perceived in free market capitalistic economies, may lead to further experimentation with significant levels of central planning of and command over economic activity.

Thinking Like an Economist

We humans relate to the resources and the people in our universe through our economic systems and institutions. The forms of ownership define our relationships to the resources, and the forms of transferring goods and services from person to person define our economic relationships with people.

There are two kinds of ownership leading to two kinds of property: privately owned private property and publicly owned (state or government owned) public property. Of course, many potentially valuable resources, such as fish in the sea and sunshine and rainfall, are originally nobody's property. But, as they become economic resources, they are captured into ownership—in the above examples—by being caught by fishermen or by shining or raining on privately owned land.

The prospect of acquiring private property, of becoming wealthy, is only by a few degrees a less urgent reason to work hard and efficiently than is survival itself. It is a fundamental expression of self-interest, and it is a basic tenet of free market economies. Grossly unequal ownership of private property, however, may lead to social disintegration and political unrest. For this reason, and to gain control of the economic process, public property is a basic tenet of centrally planned economies. Publicly owned properties do not especially evoke effective and efficient economic enterprise. They may be well managed by good and responsible public servants, and they are supposed to serve the public interest, which is why public property ownership seems appropriate for national parks and monuments, as well as for government buildings and military installations. But the potential productivity of public properties can be seriously wasted by bureaucratic bungling and even by intentional abuse and misuse. They can also become the private preserves of the politically powerful.

This leads us to the three possible kinds of economic relationships between people in the various economic institutions and systems. One is a giving relationship, such as when a parent gives tender loving care to a child or a merchant gives a free sample to a prospective customer. Another is a taking relationship, such as when a government agent collects taxes from a citizen or a criminal steals from a victim. And the third is an exchange relationship, such as when a seller and a buyer exchange goods and services for money with each other. These three relationships are summarized in the chart below.

Relationship	Active Participant	Passive Participant	Direction of Transfer	Typical Institutions
Giving:	Giver	Receiver	Giver to receiver	Families
Taking:	Taker	Person taken from	Taken-from to taker	Government
Exchange:	Both	None	Both ways	Markets

Notice that the giving relationship involves a passive participant. This undermines the effectiveness and efficiency of the relationship, because, in spite of all the best intentions and in spite of the clearest hints from the prospective recipient, a giver may not be able to discern what's best to give, how much of it to give, or when to give it. Even the most attentive mothers can't always tell where it hurts, when their infants start to cry. Finding just the right Christmas present for Aunt Emily may be even harder to do. In spite of this, giving is probably the predominant relationship in all economies, if for no other reason than that humans everywhere tend to live in some kind of family arrangement.

The taking relationship also involves a passive participant. Its efficiency is undermined by this even more, because the person being taken from, the victim, almost always loses. And even if the what, the how much, and the when of the transfer can be influenced by this involuntary participant, there is no guarantee that the taker receives more economic value than the taken-from loses.

The only relationship that promises a net gain of economic benefits—or, at least, not a loss—for both participants is exchange. Here both participants are active and voluntary. When successful, they both get more value than they give, so they often actively search each other out. We look for a store that sells what we want to buy, place an advertisement in the "classifieds" to find a buyer for what we want to sell, and send out résumés to find a good job where we can exchange our labor for a paycheck. All of which means that the exchange relationship contributes powerfully to the spirit of enterprise and economic dynamism.

No economy is or has ever been one hundred percent centrally planned or free market. But our economic system and our economic institutions powerfully determine the relationships we have with our economic resources and with other people. Within that context, each of us individually tries to do the best we can, deciding among the available alternatives and acting on them according to our moral precepts and our own self-interests. Experience and our best economic thinking seem to indicate that this can be most effectively, most efficiently, and most happily accomplished for ourselves and our families in the context of a dynamic, enterprising, mostly free market economy.

Index

The following abbreviations are used in this index: *fig* = figure or table; n = footnote; q = quote

2-4-D treatment, 89

A
acid rain, 87
addiction, 104
AFL-CIO, 81
African American families, 96
agent orange, 89
aging population, 58
Agriculture, U.S. Department of, 95-96
Aid to Families with Dependent Children, 57-58, 99
Alaska, 96
allocation, nonmarket, 38
American Federation of Labor, 81
antipoverty programs, 98-99
Asian Tigers, 113
assets, budgeting, 16-17
auto emissions, 87
automatic stabilizers, 58-59
average weekly hours in manufacturing employment, 72, 73
average weekly initial unemployment claims, 73
average weekly overtime employment, 73

B
Baer, Arthur "Bugs," 101q
Baldwin, James Arthur, 61q
banks, 63-68; big city, 63; neighborhood, 63
behavior; motives for political, 59-60; rational, 19-20

Best of Calvin and Hobbes, The, 77
bigotry, 97-98
bills, Treasury, 65
bonds, U.S. Government, 65
Boulding, Kenneth, 13q
bourgeoisie, 94
Budget of the U.S. Government, 54n
budgeting; assets, 16-17; capital, 2; resources, 16-17; time, 17
building permits for new private housing units, 73
bureaucracies, 113
business cycles, 70-71

C
capacity utilization rate, 73
capital budgeting techniques, 2
capital gains tax, 75-76
capital; human, 78; tangible, 78; workers' ownership of, 94-95
cardinal ranking, 8
Carnegie, Andrew, 95
catalytic converters, 87
cave dwellers, 85
change in business and consumer credit outstanding, 73
change in business inventories, 73
change in manufacturers' unfilled orders, 73
change in money supply M1, 73
change in sensitive materials prices, 73
charity, 98
checking accounts, 63-65
chemical spills, 84
Chicago Board of Trade, 87
cigar makers union, 80-81
circular flow of expenditures, 91, *fig91*

civil rights, 68, 98
class war, 95
Cobden, Robert, 39q
coincident indicators, 70-74
collective preference scale, 51
colonies in outer space, 85
Commerce, U.S. Department of, 75
Commonwealth of Independent States, 115
command economy, 114-115
communist; regimes, 113-115; revolution, 95
comparative advantage; law of, 40-43; theory of, 39-43
competition, 35-37; imperfect, 35-37; monopolistic, 36; perfect, 35
congestion, 84
Congress (of the United States), 44, 53, 55, 57-58, 63
Congress of Industrial Organization, 81
conservation of matter and energy, law of, 10
constant dollars, 71-72
consumer installment credit, change in, 73
consumer price index, 69
consumer sector, 74-75
consumption; of beer, 70; of pig iron, 70; personal, 73
contracts and orders for plant and equipment, 73
corn brooms, 43, 44
corporate income taxes, 53-54
corporate profits, after tax, 73, 75, 111
cost-benefit analysis, 10-11, 44, 68, 82, 102-103, 106
costs; marginal, 12, 23, 24-27, 28; variable 27-28
craft unions, 80-81
creative destructionism, 111
credit unions, 63
current dollars, 71-72

D
decision horizon, 108-109
decision makers, public, 52
decision rules, 4-5
decisions, 1-6; efficiency of, 38; environmental, 85; heroic, 1-2; incremental, 3-4, 6, 16, 19, 24, 28, 38, 43-44, 47, 60, 68, 88; individual, 50-52; marginal, 3-4, 6, 27-28; public, 50-52; threshold, 2-3, 6
defense, national, 54
delinquency rate, installment loans, 73
demand, 31-34, *fig32, fig33*; elastic, 37; for foreign exchange, 46-47; for money, 66; inelastic, 37; law of, 32, 33, 34, 88
democracy, 52, 58, 68
differentiated products, 36
diminishing marginal returns, *fig9*, 9-10, 11, 13-14, 20, 24, 26, 38
disability insurance, 80
discount rate, 67, 68
discretionary government spending, 54-57
disutility, 8
dividends, 111
Donne, John, 107q
double entry bookkeeping, 112

E
economic activity, 94-95; level of, 74-76; transformations through time, 91-92
economic development, 94
economic forecasts, 74-76
economic indicators; coincident, 70-74; lagging, 70-74; leading; 70-74; unclassified, 72-73
economic planning, 113-115, 118
economic statistics, 69-76; falsification of, 69
education, 79

efficiency; in modern economies, 111; of decisions, 38; of the market, 30
elastic demand, 37
elastic supply, 37
entitlements, 57
entropy, 91, 92; law of, 10, 18, 83-84, 90; state of, 84
environment, 19, 83-92
Environmental Protection Agency, 87
equal employment opportunity, 98
equilibrium, 17-19, 33-34, 82
estimated returns, 17
European Union, 45, 46
eventually diminishing marginal returns, *see* diminishing returns
exchange ratio, in trade, 40-41
exchange relationship, 117-118
excise taxes, 53-54
expansion, economic, 71-74
exploitation of the poor, 99-100
exports, and foreign exchange rates, 45-46
externalities, 52-53, 90; negative 86-87

F
Farm Workers of America, 81
federal budget, *fig53*, 53-59, *fig54*
federal government, 53-59
Federal Reserve System, 61, 62-68; banks, 62; Board of Governors, 63; currency, 63, 65-66
fiscal policy, 55-57, 61
fixed exchange rates, and the EU, 45
flat taxes, 75-76
flea markets, 29
Ford Motor Company, 109-110, 121
forecasts, economic, 74, 75, 76
foreign currency, 45-47
foreign exchange rates, 44-46; and imports, 45-46; and exports, 45-46
foreign sector, 74-75

Franklin, Benjamin, 7q
free trade, support for, 48
French franc, and exchange rates, 45-46
Friedman, Milton, 29q, 51

G
garbage, 84, 85, 86
Gates, Bill, 95
General Electric, 36
General Theory of Employment, Interest, and Money, The, 74
giving relationships, 116-117
global warming, 84
goals, unachievable, 19
Gompers, Samuel, 80-81
government sector, 74-75
government securities, 65, 66
gravity, law of, 10
Great Depression, 81
greed, 83, 85, 92
Gross Domestic Product (GDP), 75-76, 105
Gross National Product (GNP), 75

H
handicaps, 97-98
Hardin, Garrett, 53
Hawaii, 96
Heilbroner, Robert L., 1q, 6
help-wanted ads in newspapers, 72, 73
heroic decisions, 1-2, 6
high technology industries, 81
Hispanic families, 96
homogeneous products, 36
hours in a workday, 80
households, 91, 93, 99, 108, 109
human capital, 78
human race, survival of, 108

I
imperfect competition, 35-37
imperfect markets, 35-37
import quotas, 75-76

imports, and foreign exchange rates, 45-46
incorporation, laws of, 112
incremental decisions, 3-4, 6, 16, 19, 24, 27-28, 38, 43-44, 47, 60, 68, 88
Index of 10 Leading Indicators, 72-74
index of consumer expectations, 73
individual decisions, 50-52
individual income taxes, 53-54, 59
industrialization, 94
inelastic demand, 37, 104
inelastic supply, 37
inflation, 45, 67, 69; and poverty thresholds, 96
information, 2, 3-6, ; in decision rules, 4-5; in markets, 35-36; in rational behavior, 20; in strategies, 4-5
innocent third party, 86-89
interest rates, 66-68
interest; on federal debt, 54-55, 58
Internal Revenue Service, 110, 111
international exchange rates, *see* foreign exchange rates
international trade, 39-48, 69; opposition to, 43-44
interpersonal comparisons of value, 38
investment houses, 63
investment sector, 74-75
iron ore, 84

J

Japanese yen, and exchange rates, 45-46
Jevons, Stanley, 70
Johnson, President Lyndon, 55
joint stock companies, 112
justice, market, 38

K

Keynes, John Maynard, 49q, 74-75, 90-91

Khayyám, Omar, 83

L

lagging indicators, 70-74
large scale production, 36
law of; comparative advantage, 40-43; conservation of matter and energy, 10; demand, 32-33, 34, 88; entropy, 10, 18, 83-84, 90; eventually diminishing marginal returns, 9-10, 11, 13-14, 20, 24, 26, 38; gravity, 10; supply, 32-33, 82; thermodynamics, second, 18, 83-84
laws of incorporation, 112
leading indicators, 70-74, *fig73*
legal reserve requirements, 67
leisure, 82
Lewis, John L., 81
liability, limited, 110-111
licensing requirements, 80
limited liability, 110-111
littering, 87
Love Canal, 86

M

M1, as leading indicator, 73
M2, and index of leading indicators, 73
Mafia, 105
mandatory government spending, 54-55, 57-59
manufacturers' new orders, durable goods, 73
marginal analysis, 13-16, 22-27
marginal cost, 12, 23, 24-27, *fig25*, 28
marginal decisions, 3-4, 6, 27-28
marginal returns, 9-10, 12, 13
marginal revenue productivity, 78-79, 80
marginal revenue, 22-27, *fig25*
marginal utility, 14, 15, 16, 82
market; economy, 39, 51, 59, 106, 118; justice, 38; values, 7-8, 62

markets, 29-38; dynamics of, 34-35; efficiency of, 30; flea, 29; imperfect, 35-37; in cyberspace, 29; power of, 48
marriage, 1
Marshall, Alfred, 90-91
Marx, Karl, 90-91, 94-95
Marxist theory, 82
Marxist-Leninist communist experiment, 115
mass production industries, 81
MBAs, 111
Meals on Wheels, 98
measure of value, 62
medicaid, 54, 55, 56, 57
medicare, 54, 55, 57
medium of exchange, 62
mercantilist governments, 114
Mesabi Range, 84-85
middle class, 93-95, 96, 99-100, 101-102, 104, 105, 106
Mill, John Stuart, 90-91
minimum wage, 52, 78
Mitchell, Wesley, 70
monetary policy, 61-68
money supply M2, 73
money, 61-68; as a measure of exchange, 62; as a measure of value, 62; as a store of value, 62; borrowing of, 64-65; M1, 73; M2, 73; quantity of, 63, 66; tight, 66
monopolies, 36
mortgage debt, change in, 73
Mt. St. Helens, 90

N

NAFTA, 43
NASDAQ, 29
National Bureau of Economic Research (NBER), 70
national debt, 58
national defense, 54, 56
national income and product accounts, 75
national income, 75

Native Americans, 85
natural monopolies, 36
net business formations, 73
net change in consumer installment credit, 73
net change in mortgage debt, 73
net income, 110
new business incorporations, 73
New Deal, 81
New York Stock Exchange, 29
NICs (Newly Industrialized Countries), 113-114
noise, as pollution, 84
nonmarket allocation, 38
nonmonetary costs, 10-11
nonpriced values, 7-12

O

occupational safety, 80
oligopoly, 36
Omar Khayyám, 83q
open market policy, 65-67
opportunity costs, 10-12, 13, 38
optima, 17-19, 23, 27
ordinal rankings, 8-9
organized crime, 105
Over-The-Counter Market, 29
oxygenated gas, 87

P

partnerships, 109-110
peak, of economic activity, *fig71*
pensions, 80
perfect competition, 35
Perot, Ross, 95
perpetual motion machine, 91
personal income, 75
pig iron consumption, 70
planet earth, 85-86
planning, economic, 113-115, 118
policy, public, 38
pollution, 83-86; permits for, 87-88
population; aging, 58; movements of, 85-86

poverty 93-97; rates of children, 96; threshold, 95-96
President (of the United States), 53, 55, 57, 63
price, 7-8, 12, 29-38, 62; of economic analysis, 31; lowest, 39
prime rate, 71
primitive economies, 85
private economy, 50
private goods, 49-50
probabilities; in cost-benefit analysis, 102-103; in strategies, 5
production; large scale, 36; ratios in international trade, 40-43
products, differentiated, 36; homogeneous, 36
profit, 24-27, 111; in imperfect competition, 37; motive, 83; through international trade, 40-41
programs, social welfare, 38
progressive tax policy, 38
progressive tax, 38
proletariat, 95
proprietorships, 109-110
proprioceptors, 76
protectionists, 43-44, 48
public decision makers, 52
public decisions, 50-52
public goods, 49-50, 112
public interest, 56
public policy, 38
public utility commissions, 36

Q
quantity of money, 63, 65

R
ranking; cardinal, 8; ordinal, 8-9
rate of interest, 66-67
ratio, price to unit labor costs, 72
rational behavior, 19-20, 99, 105-106
recessions, 67, 71-74
redlining, 100
redwood trees, 84-85

relationships; exchange, 117-118; giving; 116-117; taking, 116-117
rent control, 52-53
research and development, 36
reserve requirements, 67
resource exhaustion, 84-86
resources, budgeting of, 16-17
returns; estimated, 17; marginal, 9-10, 12, 13; negative, 10; total, 9-10
revenues; marginal, 22-27; total, 28
Ricardo, David, 90-91
rights, civil, 68
risk analysis, 102-103
Rockefeller, John D., 95
Rubáiyát (of Omar Khayyám), 83

S
satisfaction, 8-9, 21
Schumpeter, Joseph, 111
second law of thermodynamics, 18, 83-84
seniority benefits, 80
share owners, 110-111
shareholders, 111
shopping; fun of, 36; malls, 30
Smith, Adam, 21q, 90-91
smog, 84-85
smokestack industries, 81
social insurance receipts, 53-54
social safety nets, 98
Social Security, 54-55, 57, 95
social welfare programs, 38
Solidarity, 114
Soviet Union, 113, 114-115
special interests; and the political process, 55, 58; opposition to trade, 43-44, 48
Special Olympics, 98
species extinctions, 84
state of entropy, 84
stock prices, 500 common stocks, 73
store of value, 62
Stout, Rex, 69q

strategies, 4-5; probabilities and, 5; specificity of, 5; uncertainties in, 5
stupidity, and environmental problems, 83, 92
substance abuse, 103-104
sulfur dioxide emissions, 87
sunspot activities, 70
supply, 31-35, *fig33*, *fig33*; elastic, 37; law of, 32-33, 82; inelastic, 37; of money, 66, *fig66*

T
taking relationship, 116-117
tangible capital, 78
tariffs, 75-76
taxes; capital gains, 75-76; corporate income, 53-54; excise, 53-54; flat, 75-76; individual income, 53-54; progressive, 59
theory of comparative advantage, 39-43
thermodynamics, second law of, 18, 83-84
third parties, innocent, 86-89
third-world countries, 113-114
threshold decisions, 2-3, 6; drawbacks of, 3; flexibility of, 3; in capital budgeting techniques, 2
Tigers, Asian, 113
tight money, 66
time, budgeting, 16
total cost, 11, 110
total profit, 25, 26
total returns, *fig9*, 9-10, 16
total revenue, 8, 22-23, 28, 110
total utility, 14-16
totalitarian control, 114-115
trade; international, 39-48; opposition to, 43-44, 48; voluntary nature of, 42
transfer payments, 57-58
Treasury, U.S., bills and bonds, 63, 65-66
trough, of economic activity, *fig71*

U
U.S. Department of Agriculture, 95-96
U.S. Department of Commerce, 75
U.S. Social Security Administration, 95
U.S. Treasury, 63; bonds and bills, 65-66
uncertainty, in strategies, 4, 27
unclassified indicators, 72-73
unemployment rates, 70, 71, 73
United Auto Workers, 81
United Mine Workers of America, 81
United States, Budget of, 54n
United Steel Workers, 81
utility, 8-9, 14-16, 17, 21; marginal, 14; negative, 8; total, 14-16
utils, 8

V
values; interpersonal comparisons of, 38; market, 7-8; measure of, 62; nonmonetary, 21; nonpriced, 7-12
variable costs, 27-28
vendor performance, 73
victimless crimes, 101, 104-105, 106
voice of the people, 51
voluntary acts, 29-30, 39, 42-43
volunteer work, 98

W
wages, 70, 80-81
Walesa, Lech, 114
water table, 84-85
wealth; and independence, 77; as a motive, 115-116; as a source of income, 78
welfare; effects of international trade, 41-42; dependency on, 99; social programs for, 38
work, and income, 78-80
working conditions, 80
workweek, hours of, 82
world-wide web sites, 76